T0386306

SANJAY AGGARWAL

photography by Dan Jones

Spice Kitchen

Vibrant Recipes and Spice Blends for the Home Cook

Hardie Grant

QUADRILLE

For Mum - I owe you everything x

Contents

Foreword

Growing up in India, I spent so much time in the kitchen alongside my mum, my aunties and my sisters learning how to cook with spices. There were always women around me: making food, talking, laughing and sharing the work. Everything I do in my kitchen to this day, I can trace back to those special times in my family back home.

Moving to the UK after I got married was life-changing for me in so many ways: the weather, the culture and, of course, the food. Being separated from my family was tough, and cooking the meals that reminded me of them kept me connected to my roots. And in time, the familiar smell of cumin seeds toasting in my kitchen, the aromas of spices being blended in my pestle and mortar, and the meals I prepared all helped me to build a foundation for my own home and growing family.

From this foundation, a world of flavour and opportunity began to open up to me. Birmingham was a bustling foodie paradise, and it turns out, the perfect place for me to have landed. I slowly made my connections and found growers and suppliers of the foods I loved, and also learned new cuisines from the people around me. Suddenly I was learning about Middle Eastern, Moroccan, Mexican and Italian traditions. And ironically, it was my neighbour who first taught me how to make a biryani, as it wasn't something my family ate back home in India!

Life for me has always centred around food: it's definitely how I show love to my family, and I can't remember a day of my adult life when I haven't cooked something. My home has always had an open door to any extended family members wanting to come and build a life in the UK, and the first thing we would do after their long trip from India was sit together at our kitchen table and share a big pot of food, while we talked of their hopes and dreams for the future. That dining table has been the springboard for so many new beginnings, all the more special with a lovingly made family meal.

It's the very same dining table that my son Sanjay and I sat at when we came up with the idea for our little family business - Spice Kitchen - back in 2012. Naturally, any business we set up was always going to involve spices, and now, in my seventh decade, I am so happy to be sharing my passion for food with people all around the world.

But, what I love the most about all of this is that I have been able to pass on everything I learned back home in India to Sanjay. The knowledge of spice I was fortunate to have been taught all those years ago, by those amazing women, is now being carried forward in this book. Sanjay watched me in the kitchen with a keen eye, he asked questions and I quickly realized he had a gift for understanding food and how to balance flavour. He used to tell me what spice, seasoning or ingredient was missing from a dish from a very young age... and I knew from that point he was going to be a keen foodie!

Sanjay has taken what he learned from watching me in the kitchen and made it relevant to the modern day. By using simple spice blends instead of long lists of ingredients, people no longer need hours and hours to cook beautiful food for their families.

The recipes you will discover in this book have flavour in abundance, but more than that, they carry with them little echoes of our family history. In even the simplest of recipes, you will taste the wisdom of my ancestors who, all those years ago, diligently taught me how to blend and cook with spices. This book has come through my ancestors, to me, then to Sanjay, and now to you. All with love.

Shashi

Introduction

My mum has spent her life lovingly cooking with spices. Her treasured 100-year-old spice grinder was once her mother's. After being born in Kenya she moved to India, and was the first of our entire family to move to the UK from India after she got married. Living in another country felt like a whole new world to her, and her spice grinder connected her to home. She treasured it and used it daily to make the blends her mum had taught her to make when she was growing up.

I understand that the spice grinder was made in the 1900s, but that it was most likely intended to be a coffee grinder. By landing with our family in Kenya and then being moved to India, the spice grinder took on a different purpose and over the years has helped our family to grind huge amounts of spices and blends. Fast-forward to the 1970s when Mum moved to the UK, the spice grinder's role diversified yet again. As Mum's food world evolved through new people and influences, and the big food culture in Birmingham at that time, the spice grinder was there every step of the way to deliver gorgeous blends inspired by Middle Eastern, Moroccan and Chinese food traditions. As an object, the spice grinder represents our multicultural world and was even the inspiration for our little family business, Spice Kitchen.

The family's spice grinder remains one of the most important tools Mum owns: so much of the work done in her kitchen is in preparing her spice blends, and you can't beat the flavour from freshly ground spices. When I was growing up, our house was always filled with the amazing aromas of Indian or Middle Eastern cooking and we ate food cooked with spices almost every day. Mum was always busy making plenty of blends in advance,

to save herself time, and these would provide the backbone of what we ate. To this day, every month, on a Sunday, she still makes a big batch of her grandmother's garam masala - a phrase that literally translates as 'spice blend' using her trusted spice grinder.

Following her retirement a decade ago, Mum was searching for a project that would keep her busy (there's no way she was ever going to retire!) and our little family business Spice Kitchen was born. All those spice blends she had used at home, and gifted to friends and family, were made available - it's possible you may have some of these in your own kitchen. Her blends are so reliable, so adaptable and always delicious; the best and easiest way to add bags of flavour to whatever it is she's cooking. I've taken this knowledge - together with a love of spice and a genuine enjoyment of experimenting with flavour - from her kitchen into mine, and I'm now passing it on to my own daughter.

I have always been a flavour junkie. Having eaten curries almost from the day I was born (even the baked beans I ate as a child were always spiced), food without spice isn't even food to me! In fact, I used to carry spices in my pockets when I went out to a restaurant, so I could sneak flavour into my meal. Spice blends are now my go-to way of introducing flavour and I fully believe that they can make cooking easier.

Despite this, when I suggested to Mum that I wanted to write a book about using blends instead of whole spices, even she was dubious. She was unsure that the flavour would be the same. But, after she recreated her incredible Street Style Pav Bhaji recipe with a blend, she was amazed. I love that, in her seventh decade, Mum is still prepared to be open minded and try new things. The cooking styles and methods I am going to introduce to you represent this evolution in how I now cook for my family. And, it's this approach that I want to suggest you take into your own kitchen too. I'm confident that, if you have a spice blend in your cupboard or drawer, you're already halfway to dinner! It doesn't even have to be one of Spice Kitchen's spice blends; supermarket shelves and local stores are lined with them, and I'm willing to bet you have one or two sitting around, relegated, unloved and underused.

The accessibility of spices in the UK, along with other parts of the western world, has altered significantly since they were first introduced. Once the privilege of the upper classes and a symbol of the colonial spread of Britain across the globe, spices are now widely accessible. When black pepper was first imported it was known as black gold, becoming more common in European kitchens in the 18th century, while today it probably sits alongside salt on your kitchen table, or next to your hob, ready to crack into every dish. Because of this ubiquity, it's estimated that 20 per cent of today's spice trade is made up of black pepper.

With this book, I want to help you to be as confident using spice blends as you are with black pepper. Along the way, I want to demystify cooking with spices, to reassure you that you don't need endless time, fancy equipment or a full pantry, and to show you how to make amazing meals that will become your family's go-to favourites for years to come. Mum's chickpea curry using our garam masala blend is adored by our whole family who ask for it every time we get together - even the team at Spice Kitchen now makes a request for a batch every time she visits. In fact, if you're ever in Birmingham, you should look her up and demand a bowl!

But this book isn't just about recreating the old favourites. I also want to empower you to experiment and to provide you with some special 'Spice Freedom' recipes that allow you to play around and trust your own tastebuds. 'Spice Freedom' takes one dish and shows how, by switching the blend, you can open a world of flavour possibilities.

I know you're busy, so the book has been structured to give you ideas and inspiration depending on the time you have available. This is also why you won't find long lists of ingredients in our recipes: instead I offer you dishes that can be created using a simple blend. There's recipes for quick lunches, for midweek meals, for special occasions, for Sunday lunch and for big messy feasts where everyone helps themselves - the way both Mum and I cook in our homes. Every chapter is filled with our family favourites and includes a range of ideas for all tastes and dietary demands. Mum is a lifelong vegetarian, so there is plenty here for veggies - and vegans too.

This is the sort of food I love to cook, want to eat, and feast on with friends and family; all made better with spice. And, for those of you who want to go a step further, I'm excited to share with you a range of simple spice blends you can make in your kitchen at home, from scratch.

I hope you enjoy.

With love,
Sanjay x

Equipment

You don't need to invest in loads of fancy equipment to get the best out of this book, but there are some basic kitchen gadgets and utensils that are going to make your life so much easier. You don't have to spend a fortune either - do try one of the online auction sites for some great pre-loved bargains. Here's a quick overview of what to look out for.

Baking trays (sheets) A couple of decent-sized baking trays (pans) will serve you well. I always try to line mine with baking paper to prevent ingredients from sticking and also to help with the washing-up mission at the end of the meal! A decent cake tin (pan) for making tarts is always useful to have. Try to go for one around 20cm (8in) diameter and if you can, choose a tin with a loose bottom to make removing tarts and cakes easier.

Clean jars for storing spice blends, pickles and dips You will be learning how to make spice blends and loads of amazing chutneys, pickles and dips as you work through this book. It makes life so much easier if you have a stash of clean jars ready to use. Go for a variety of sizes but try to choose glass where possible so you can see what's inside! You can sterilize clean jars by rinsing them with boiling water and then drying them off in the oven at 120°C fan/140°C/275°F/gas mark 1 for 10 minutes, or in a microwave on high setting for 30-45 seconds.

Coffee grinder A weird inclusion in a book about spices? Actually, no. A basic coffee grinder will become your best friend if you decide to go down the route of making your own spice blends. They are great for blitzing up whole spices, take much less effort than a pestle and mortar and will ensure a consistent texture for your blends.

Digital scales Reliable scales are obviously useful for weighing ingredients and making sure you're accurately following recipes, but particularly for the spice blends in this book. A set of digital scales can be purchased cheaply online, so if you intend on making your own blends, it's definitely worth this small investment.

Heavy-bottomed frying pans (skillets) and saucepans with well-fitting (glass) lids The term 'heavy-bottomed pan' is quite possibly the most-used phrase in this book! It's key for so many of the recipes that you need at least one, if not two, pans that have a decent base and a tight-fitting lid. Ingredients are less likely to stick or burn and everything just cooks - and therefore tastes - so much better.

Ice-cream scoop Simply because everyone needs an ice-cream scoop in their lives!

Ice-cube trays Get yourself a good stash of these as you're going to be freezing ginger-garlic paste, sauces, herbs and much more so that you have things ready prepared.

Labels Label and date everything immediately, whether it's spice blends or sauces in freezer bags. It's so frustrating to make something and then not recognize it two months later!

Measuring jugs/cups I prefer glass because it cleans up better: plastic will tarnish, and also the measuring lines tend to rub off with continued use.

Mixing bowls Aim for a range of sizes. I tend to use glass or ceramic as they are heat- and dishwasher-safe, but also because plastic bowls will pick up some of the colour from the spice.

Pestle and mortar You can pick up second-hand pestle and mortars cheaply online. It's up to you what to go for but my advice would be to invest in a heavy one - ideally made of granite or stone - with

a heavy pestle. The pestle has one job in life: to smash things up, so you want to find one that is really robust that you feel confident in.

Stick blender and food processor Both these gadgets make life so much easier when you're blending sauces or making pastes. Hand-held stick blenders are far cheaper and great for fine blending; however, a food processor offers you so much more functionality, like shredding veggies, or making dough and pastry.

Tupperware For leftovers and freezing sauces and chutneys. Once you get into batch cooking and freezing ahead of time, you can never have enough, I promise. One trick I learned when buying Tupperware is to always buy the same containers because lids go missing! So if you have all of the same container in the same size, you'll never end up too short of lids. Also, for a cheaper option, save takeaway containers too, if they are decent quality.

Utensils Good-quality sharp knives in a range of sizes, decent wooden spoons, teaspoons and tablespoons for measuring your spices are all going to come in handy.

On a really serious note

This book is about flavour. It's about experimentation, fun and getting stuck in. It's about trying out spice blends and tasting the complexity and richness that they bring to ingredients. I love food, I want to celebrate it and enjoy it, and I want that for you too.

But this book exists against a backdrop of something much bigger.

Some of the dishes in this book have a rich cultural heritage and I've been so mindful of this when writing it. I am very aware that I am, in many ways, tampering with tradition with the mere suggestion that a spice blend can replicate the complex and rich flavour achieved when using single or whole spices. Mum raised an eyebrow when I said it, and I'm sure there will be many more eyebrows raised along the way. It's a big deal to challenge heritage and history, and not one I've embarked on lightly. From my vantage point, I've been able to play around and challenge traditions. Despite my jovial and often flippant tone, honouring tradition and making my ancestors proud is so important to me, but it's also bigger than me: we are at a crucial moment on the world stage where cultural appropriation and respect are huge topics.

Spices are by virtue of my upbringing a staple part of our home kitchen. Growing up, no cooking in Mum's kitchen would have happened without spices. Even with this in mind, and having run Spice Kitchen for a decade, eating my way around the world (literally twice, for two years), I am still awestruck with how much I learn every day.

Food has massively changed over the 50 years since my mum came to the UK. I was born and raised in Birmingham, I've been travelling on two world trips and went off to university, all the while being influenced along the way. In my own lifetime, so much has changed in terms of how we cook, and I am bringing a cookbook to the table that reflects all of this. Our diverse cultural influences and family heritage, including a migration story, means it is difficult to separate what is authentic, what is traditional and what is adapted. Ultimately it doesn't really matter; all I can say for sure is that the food I hope to share with you is incredibly tasty!

The recipes in this book represent how I cook, in my kitchen, with blends, and living in an ever-evolving, blended world. As you take these recipes forward and cook with them, they too will take on a life of their own and evolve according to your tastebuds, your preferences, your family, your life.

That is the way it always should be and, in truth, the way it has always been.

Store-cupboard essentials

The benefits of a fully stocked store cupboard cannot be overstated. That said, the way you stock your cupboard depends largely on the types of dishes you want to make. It would be unrealistic to suggest we can prepare you for every eventuality, but this section aims to give you a good start. So, to get you properly prepared for success with our book and our way of cooking, we suggest you invest in some of the following:

Black pepper - for me it's peppercorns all the way, rather than the pre-ground version.

Canned chickpeas (garbanzo beans) and kidney beans - great for homemade hummus but also perfect for making a curry when you don't have time to soak dried peas and beans overnight.

Canned tomatoes - the basis of so many dishes and a key feature in this book. We tend to go for good-quality plum tomatoes but chopped work equally well.

Coconut milk - I always go for full-fat but using reduced-fat is OK. A stock of coconut milk will mean you can easily knock up a super-tasty curry in no time at all.

Cornflour (cornstarch) - great for quickly thickening up sauces and also for coating ingredients such as tofu or chicken breasts.

Oils - it's worth having several in your cupboard. I always make sure I have good-quality olive oil, extra virgin olive oil, sunflower, vegetable and rapeseed (canola) oil. Many of the recipes in this book use sunflower or vegetable oil, so if you buy a big bottle it will serve you well.

Flour - I use a lot of self-raising (self-rising) flour, especially to make quick and easy midweek naan bread. I also keep a good stash of '00' flour, plain (all-purpose), and strong bread flour.

Ground turmeric - we do sometimes suggest turmeric as an optional ingredient in our ingredients list. It's great for quickly adding colour and flavour to your dishes and also super healthy too.

Honey - a simple drizzle transforms a lowly baked feta into the stuff of dreams. Honey is non-negotiable on this list!

Lemon and lime juice - literally life-changing! It's so frustrating to have all the ingredients for a recipe and then find out you're missing a lemon or lime. Get yourself some in a bottle and never go short again.

Lentils - most supermarkets now sell black urad lentils, which you need for dals; do also pick up some split chickpeas (chana dal) and red lentils for soups and stews generally.

Noodles - egg or rice noodles are fine; we're also fans of udon noodles, which are great for vegans.

Nuts, seeds and dried fruits - where you can, grab sesame, nigella and onion seeds, as well as dried fruits such as dates, prunes and apricots.

Passata (strained tomatoes) - I use bottles and bottles of passata for the same reason as canned tomatoes: they are the bedrock of so many dishes and a really great way to quickly knock up a sauce.

Rice - choose good-quality basmati rice to accompany your curries and stir fries.

Salt - my preference is always to go for flaky sea salt because it can add great texture when crunched over dishes.

Sugar - despite the health warnings, sometimes only a spoonful of sugar will do. White, granulated sugar is fine for most of the recipes in this book. If you prefer brown then just stock up on what you prefer.

Tacos and tortillas - these last for ages and so it's worth picking them up when you're at the shops and saving them for a rainy day.

Making use of your freezer

This is no exaggeration: Mum can knock up a meal for 20 people in an hour without feeling remotely rushed or stressed. Our family think she's some sort of wizard, but actually it's all down to how well she uses her freezer to get prepared in advance. With any spare time or spare ingredients, she'll be in the kitchen making the best use out of what she's got and saving herself time later down the line. Even in her 'retirement' this is her approach, but it was especially important to her when she had three young children. When I asked her about this, she said: 'As a working mum with three children under 10, I was always aware of how little time I had. Cooking for the family was a little more complicated as I am vegetarian but everyone else eats meat, so there was always some adapting to do. Using my freezer to prepare and get ahead meant I could easily pull together a tasty meal that everyone enjoyed.'

Mum is not only the most organized home cook I've ever met, but she's also the most frugal and I think this is a huge driver for her in making sure she gets the most out of anything she cooks or chops. Given the amount of food waste we produce in the UK alone, I reckon more of us could take a leaf out of her book and get smart about how we prepare ingredients and use our freezers.

I took a peek into Mum's freezer on a random day when I was writing this book and here is what I found:

Various chutneys - spiced tomato, zingy mint and coriander (cilantro) and tamarind - frozen into ice-cube trays. She pops them out of their trays about an hour before serving a meal for hassle free dips.

Cooked onions - browned in oil for about 15 minutes and then frozen ready to pop into a biryani or pav bhaji.

Diced onions - for dals, curries, soups, tagines and stews. Mum will simply get them out a few hours before she needs them, defrost, and be ready to cook without the obligatory onion chopping regime!

Ginger-garlic and green chilli pastes - frozen into ice-cube trays ready to defrost and add to curries and tagines when needed.

Urad lentils, chickpeas (garbanzo beans) and kidney beans - presoaked and pressure cooked, then, once cooled, sealed in freezer bags ready for use in whatever she's cooking.

Dal makhani, tarka and other sauces - frozen into individual portions, so she can get them out in the morning for dinner later on.

Fresh herbs from the market or garden, mixed with butter or veg oil and frozen into ice-cube trays. For her, being frugal as she is, this is a great way to cut down on waste too.

Frozen meat, fish and veggies - such as chicken, haddock or cod, and vegetables such as peas, spinach and carrots. Mum is a big fan of 'use what you have' rather than sticking religiously to a recipe and so a good stash of frozen staples means she can rustle up veggie meals for herself while having plenty of options for the meat eaters.

Pre-made bread dough - for naan bread, pitta, flatbreads and other baking missions!

Leftovers in Tupperware - if ever there is anything left after the family meal, Mum always freezes what's left for another day. She always writes what's in the container on the lid and puts the date on there too so she can easily identify what she's got.

Leftover coconut milk - if a recipe requires half a can, Mum will freeze the rest in a Tupperware container and find a use for it another day.

Filo (phyllo) and other pastries - that she will take out and defrost a few hours in advance, ready to make a delicious pie or tart. When she moved from India Mum learned how to make loads of delicious veggie pies and they have become a staple in her diet ever since.

Spice blends: a world of flavour

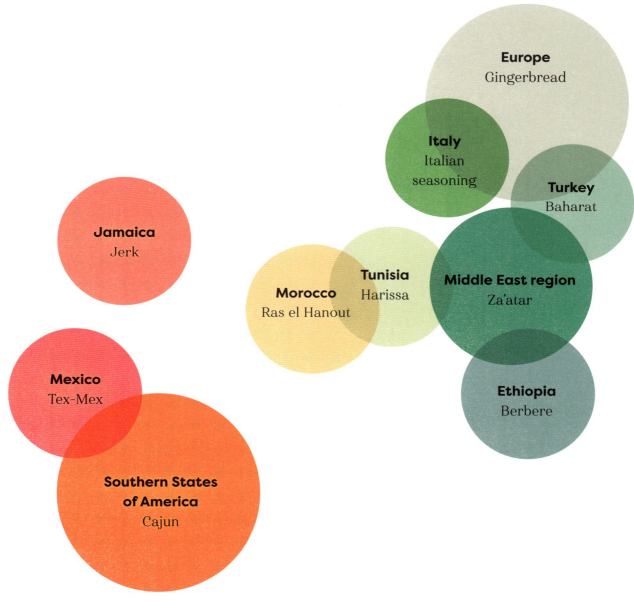

Jamaica
Jerk

Mexico
Tex-Mex

Southern States
of America
Cajun

Europe
Gingerbread

Italy
Italian
seasoning

Turkey
Baharat

Morocco
Ras el Hanout

Tunisia
Harissa

Middle East region
Za'atar

Ethiopia
Berbere

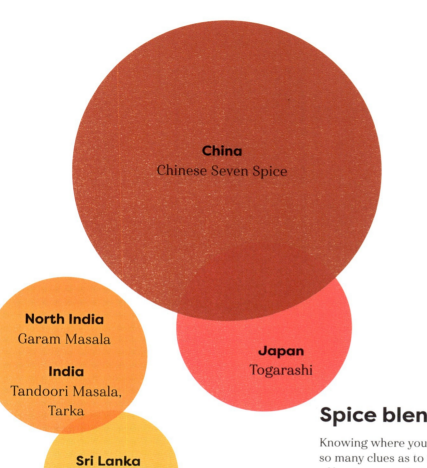

China
Chinese Seven Spice

North India
Garam Masala

India
Tandoori Masala,
Tarka

Japan
Togarashi

Sri Lanka
Sri Lankan Curry
Powder

Spice blend origins

Knowing where your blends originated can give so many clues as to their potential flavour, level of heat or even their best use. Simply by knowing garam masala is an Indian blend, we can hazard an (educated) guess that it's going to be awesome in a curry. Similarly, we can easily make the connection between Tex-Mex and the lovely zingy freshness of lime and coriander (cilantro). We might, however, be surprised to learn that gingerbread hails from the UK and across Europe!

Here's a brief overview of what you need to know about spice blends to get started. But worry not... I'm not going to ask you to become a spice connoisseur (but I won't stop you if that's your bag) and I don't expect you to remember all (or any!) of this. I'm also reluctant to get all flouncy with foodie words that no one actually uses in conversations with friends, so I'm definitely going to keep this real! Having said that, I do believe it's good to have a bit of knowledge up your sleeve as to the types of flavours you're adding to your dishes when you use a spice blend. It helps you know what to avoid and can also help you to replicate what you love.

Baharat

Overview: Baharat is a spice blend with Middle Eastern origins. The word 'baharat' itself means 'spice' in Arabic.

Origins: Originally hailing from Aleppo, Syria, the spiciness of this blend results from the inclusion of Aleppo pepper. While baharat is thought to originate from Syria, it is also used widely in Turkey and Saudi Arabia.

Uses: Baharat can be a dry rub for meat before it is barbecued or grilled, added to marinades and used as a seasoning at the end of cooking to add flavour to dishes.

Flavour profile: Sweet, smoky, aromatic, warming and earthy.

Spice level: Mild.

Availability: Widely available.

Cajun

Overview: Originally hailing from Louisiana, this is a rustic mix of staple spices such as cumin, coriander, paprika and oregano.

Origins: Believed to have developed in the south of America in the 18th century.

Uses: Great for barbecues (grills), brilliant for adding a flavour punch to fries or wedges. Also really useful as a rub for meat, chicken, vegetables or tofu.

Flavour profile: Bold, spicy and earthy.

Spice level: Medium (our recipe is a little milder than most, so please feel free to spice it up if you like more heat).

Availability: Widely available.

Berbere

Overview: An absolute staple in many Ethiopian kitchens. The blend almost always includes paprika, chilli, cardamom and ginger. You'll find it in the Doro Wot recipe in this book on page 105.

Origins: Initially originated from North Africa.

Uses: Great in stews and for spicing up meatballs, perfect for adding a real depth of flavour to vegetable and bean dishes.

Flavour profile: Since berbere contains many ingredients, each with its unique flavour, there isn't one 'standard' flavour. However, what you will find - and what you will see from our spice blend recipe (see page 25) - is a lovely mix of heat from the chilli and a balanced and zingy warmth from the ginger.

Spice level: Medium.

Availability: Widely available online and in supermarkets.

Chinese Seven Spice

Overview: A lovely fragrant blend of spices that packs a flavourful punch. You have to taste this to understand why it's so popular in Chinese cooking.

Origins: Originally a blend of five spices, what we refer to as a Chinese spice blend has its origins in traditional Chinese medicine. The blend was originally considered to balance 'yin' and 'yang' energies and to promote overall good health.

Uses: Great in stir-fries, as a rub for crispy duck, and with other fatty meats such as pork or goose.

Flavour profile: This blend smells so good and is a lovely balance of sweet, bitter, sour, salty and savoury. You might notice a slight numbing sensation in your mouth from the Szechuan peppers. I recommend you try one Szechuan peppercorn on its own (all of my team at Spice Kitchen have been subject to this rite of passage) to get a sense of this: some people love it and others don't. If you're not a fan, you can leave them out when you come to make your spice blend.

Spice level: Mild yet warming.

Availability: Chinese or any supermarket and online.

Garam Masala

Overview: Garam masala translates as 'hot spice mix', although it's more warm than hot. There is no single recipe as ingredients vary depending on the region, and the preferences of families. Our blend is one we've kept secret for seven generations, and we love it. Mum lived in Ludhiana, Punjab, and so the recipe is very much rooted in this region.

Origins: Originally from North India it is also used in Pakistan, Sri Lanka, Bangladesh and Nepal.

Uses: Widely used in many Indian dishes, including samosas, lentil dishes and a broad range of curries. It can also be added at the end of cooking as a seasoning to add additional flavour to a dish.

Flavour profile: Warming, sweet, floral, with a touch of heat.

Spice level: Mild to medium. A blend from southern parts of India will be hotter.

Availability: Widely available.

Gingerbread (Speculaas)

Overview: Gingerbread has a delicious aroma as well as a memorable taste. Our recipe in this book (page 26) is a hybrid of the traditional gingerbread and the European version - Speculaas - which has both Belgian and Germanic roots.

Origins: It is believed that around 2400 BCE, the Greeks and Egyptians developed a recipe for gingerbread for use in religious ceremonies.

Uses: The most obvious use is in baking, especially cookies, cakes, truffles and even smoothies. We love gingerbread in hot chocolate and brownies, and you'll find recipes for both in this book. It also works really well in a latte and as a flavouring for ice cream.

Flavour profile: The very familiar taste of childhood treats! Sweet, warming and mildly spiced.

Spice level: Warming but not spicy.

Availability: Available online; check local supermarkets.

Harissa

Overview: Harissa is a blend of smoking-hot peppers and spices and is widely used in North African and Middle Eastern cooking, particularly in Tunisia, Algeria, Morocco and Libya. Ingredients vary according to regions and even towns, meaning hundreds of recipes are out there!

Origins: Harissa is believed to have originated in Tunisia, where nowadays it is used like ketchup or mustard in sauce form as a condiment.

Uses: Great for spicing up any and every dish if you're a chilli lover, especially curries and stews! It's easily the most-used spice blend in this book, even in our Spiced-up Bloody Mary (see page 178). It can also be used as a condiment.

Flavour profile: Totally addictive! It's fiery, peppery and smoky all at the same time.

Spice level: Hot.

Availability: Widely available.

Italian Seasoning

Overview: Italian cooks often use fresh herbs instead of dried, but for convenience and availability, dried is fine. The main herbs in Italian seasoning vary widely according to region, but basil, oregano, marjoram, rosemary and thyme feature in most.

Origins: Likely ancient Greece or Rome. The blend of herbs that we refer to today as 'Italian seasoning' originated in the Mediterranean region. The blend of herbs in our recipe here is more authentically Tuscan.

Uses: As a seasoning for vegetables and meat, or to enliven dishes such as pasta, bolognese, lasagne and pizza. Rub the dried herbs between your palms when you add to dishes, as this action releases the oils and gives a better flavour.

Flavour profile: Savoury, floral, beautifully aromatic and sometimes pungent.

Spice level: None!

Availability: Widely available in supermarkets and online.

Jerk

Overview: Jerk is the name of a spice blend but also a style of cooking that is specific to Jamaica. It is a complex blend of ingredients: I use 12 spices in the Jerk blend in this book and some chefs use more. The fire in this blend comes from the cayenne pepper but is balanced nicely with sweetness from the sugar and allspice.
Origins: Jerk is integral to Jamaican history and can be traced as far back as the mid-17th century.
Uses: A brilliant rub for any meat or vegetables, lovely with the extra smokiness from a barbecue (grill). Jerk chicken is obviously legendary and is something we all have to try at least once.
Flavour profile: Fragrant, savoury, sweet, spicy.
Spice level: Medium to hot.
Availability: Widely available in stores and online.

Mexican (Tex-Mex)

Overview: Mexico is famous for its big flavours, as well as the complexity of its cuisine. I've travelled across Mexico and have seen the complex dishes made there. The Mexican blend in this book is a simplified - actually non-authentic - mix of flavours that are more 'Tex-Mex' than traditional Mexican.
Origins: You can find Mexican spice blends almost anywhere and yet they actually come from nowhere in particular! Spices are a key part of Mexican cuisine that goes beyond a simple seasoning or rub.
Flavour profile: Using smoked or unsmoked paprika makes a significant difference to the flavour. Some people don't like smoky paprika, so if you're making the spice blend, choose which you prefer. You can also add smokiness to the dish by the way you cook, so griddling and barbecuing will add an injection of smoke.
Uses: The most obvious uses are, of course, in fajitas, tacos and burritos; however, we've included a lovely Tex-Mex burger in this book to bring an America-meets-Mexico angle.
Spice level: Medium to hot.
Availability: Very widely available.

Ras el Hanout

Overview: Ras el Hanout means 'head of the spice shop' in Arabic. The blend is a mixture of both herbs and spices. As head of my own little spice shop, I utilize 16 ingredients, including rose petals. In Morocco I saw so many people growing rose petals for use in Ras, and I had to reflect this.
Origins: This complex blend has its roots in Moroccan history. As a critical gateway for goods moving from Africa to Europe, Morocco was pivotal in the spice trade. Spices from all over the world became part of Moroccan cuisine and you will see this reflected in the broad range of spices included in the blend.
Uses: Brilliant as a marinade or rub for meat and veggies. Lovely in tagines and stews.
Flavour profile: Woody, pungent and bitter.
Spice level: Mild.
Availability: Widely available.

Sri Lankan Curry Powder

Overview: This spice blend is distinctive for the bright colour it will add to your dishes.
Origins: Sri Lankan cuisine shares close links with other South and South-east Asian food and as such includes many non-native ingredients as a result of international trading. Despite this, Sri Lankan curry powder offers a distinct taste that is definitely evocative of the island's culture and cuisine.
Uses: Perfect for curries, lovely with fish as it doesn't overpower the delicate flavours.
Flavour profile: Sri Lankan curries tend to be spicy, which is why I love them so much. The inclusion of the incredible curry leaf (see page 23) offers the distinct flavour you will associate with a curry.
Spice level: Medium to hot (however, people do often add more heat to their blends depending on their preference).
Availability: Widely available online and in most supermarkets.

Tandoori Masala

Overview: This blend almost universally includes cumin, coriander and turmeric. You'll probably know that 'Tandoori' meat or vegetables are distinctively bright in colour; however, this is only down to food colouring. The tandoori blend you'll find in the next chapter uses beetroot powder to add the same colour but without the additives. If you can't get hold of beetroot powder, add tomato purée (paste) for an injection of colour.

Origins: Believed to have been invented as late as the 1920s in Pakistan, the Tandoori spice blend was originally created for use in a tandoor (clay oven).

Uses: Great for barbecues (grills) or as a rub for meat.

Flavour profile: Aromatic, rich and spicy.

Spice level: Medium.

Availability: Widely available.

Togarashi

Overview: Often referred to as 'seven-spice powder' Togarashi is used widely in Japanese cuisine.

Origins: It is believed that togarashi dates back to around the 17th century, when it was first traded in a little fishing village called Edo, which we now know as Tokyo.

Uses: Great as a rub for meat, vegetables and seafood, traditionally used as a sprinkle for finishing a cooked dish and adding flavour at the end of cooking. Works brilliantly in ramen dishes and with tofu.

Flavour profile: Adds a lovely sweet, umami flavour to dishes. Can be smoky too.

Spice level: Mild to medium.

Availability: Increasingly popular and available in supermarkets and online.

Tarka

Overview: Mustard seeds and cumin are the bedrock of so many Indian dishes and they are the key ingredients in this simple yet flavourful combo.

Origins: 'Tarka' refers to the process of tempering or frying spices in oil so that their flavour is released. In my family we refer to this simple mix of whole spices as our 'Tarka Blend' as we know that the easy combination of just two spices will make a massive difference to the overall flavour of a dish.

Uses: This blend is best suited for flavouring the oil at the start of your cooking, and the most distinct thing you'll notice is that the moment your blend hits the pan, your kitchen is filled with that distinct aroma of a curry house. This is definitely the cumin talking!

Flavour profile: Mustard seeds are pretty bitter and the cumin is earthy and warming, so as a pairing they pack a real flavourful punch.

Spice level: Warming but not spicy.

Availability: It's super easy to buy cumin and mustard seeds.

Za'atar

Overview: Za'atar is best known for its use in Middle Eastern and Mediterranean cooking. As with many spice blends, exactly what is in za'atar varies from region to region. Typically, it will include sesame seeds, oregano and thyme. We love to include sumac for a salty pop.

Origins: Interestingly, za'atar links back to the 12th century in Levantine (Eastern Mediterranean) culture, making it pretty ancient in terms of world spice blends!

Uses: Great for grilled and roasted vegetables and also lovely as a seasoning for salads. I especially love it served simply on fresh tomatoes.

Flavour profile: Herby, nutty and crunchy (thanks to the sesame seeds).

Spice level: Mild.

Availability: This blend is becoming more widely known and available in UK supermarkets; check online if you can't find it.

How to make your own spice blends

I want to empower you to make amazing food, so if making blends from scratch is your bag, read on. If not, or you're time-poor, please feel free to skip this chapter: all the blends I've included here are widely available. For those of you who do have the time, patience and inclination to make your own blends, I will show you how. It's fun to do, your house will smell amazing, and the whole experience will bring you closer to your ingredients. Either way, you're going to make delicious dishes.

A single spice - or herb - can transform and elevate the humblest of recipes. Think black pepper on your carbonara, smoked paprika dusted on your homemade slaw, or oregano scrunched into your bolognese. With spice blends, though, I'm talking about adding flavour on another level entirely. The blends you will learn to make and cook with in this book will bring a rich complexity and a depth of flavour to your dishes with the same ease and simplicity as when you add black pepper or oregano to your food.

At their core, spice blends are a simple selection of spices - nothing more complex than that. But at the same time, you will be taking your tastebuds on a real adventure and eating your way around the globe. Once you know how to make your own spice blends, a world of flavour is available to you.

Spice blends vary widely according to different tastes and local availability of ingredients: this might be other regions in their country of origin or different recipes that have evolved within families.

There are also different methods for making blends and I want to address one of these here. Dry-roasting spices before blending - for example - is vital in spice cultivation. Spices are often freshly picked and then dry-roasted to stop them from going mouldy, especially in India. However, the spices you are going to buy in stores and supermarkets will have already been dried, so there is no moisture left in them. For this reason, I'm not asking you to dry-roast your spices before blending them. This makes your life easy and also means you're less likely to over-roast or burn your spices, which can impact the flavour of your food.

What you need

Spices

You can use ground (powdered) or whole spices to make your blends. All versions work equally well - you can even go for a combination of both ground and whole. Grab what's available and don't stress.

Here's a quick guide to our terminology when making blends:

In the spice blend recipes, I name the spice, for example, 'cumin', which leaves you free to use cumin seeds or ground cumin. Use what you have. The specific recipe will guide you as to what to do depending on whether you have whole seeds/spices or ground. I never recommend that you use fresh ingredients such as turmeric, ginger, onions or garlic: these are always powder or granules.

Occasionally, you'll notice I ask that you leave ingredients whole, for instance, in the Togarashi recipe, the sesame seeds are not ground with the other ingredients but instead added at the end. Where this is the case, I will say so in the recipe method.

When I say coriander, I mean the seeds or ground coriander, not the fresh leaves that are used as a herb (cilantro)! Likewise, when I mention herbs such as parsley, thyme, oregano and basil, I mean the dried varieties.

When I say peppercorns, I mean black pepper.

If you see fenugreek listed, it's the seeds and not the leaves.

For cardamom, I am always referring to green cardamom seeds (that are within the pods) or the whole pods.

A note on curry leaves

I also want to mention curry leaves: they are an incredible ingredient, so if you see them fresh, buy them and freeze them for when you need them. Even better, get yourself a curry plant and grow your own. Mum transported hers from Kenya in her suitcase and it is thriving in her garden in Birmingham to this day. They bring a flavour to your dishes that you can't replicate.

Equipment

You will need a coffee grinder or a good-quality pestle and mortar (see Equipment on page 8 for details on these). The advantage of using a pestle and mortar is that you can keep grinding until you get the consistency you want, whereas with a coffee grinder, you have less control over the coarseness of your blend. If you're a fan of a really consistent blend, then use a coffee grinder, as this will give you a smoother end result.

Many people worry that by using a coffee grinder, the spices will get warm and therefore the flavour will be impaired. I've never known this to happen, so please don't worry: you won't ruin your dishes - just use whatever method works for you.

Labels

Don't make the mistake of using precious spices in a blend and then not recognizing what it is in a month's time! Get some labels and write the blend's name on the jar, together with the date you made it. Try to have a periodic clearout so you don't use old, out-of-date blends in your recipes.

Quantities and storage

Each blend recipe in this chapter makes 100g (3½oz). There are no equivalents in ounces for the spices because I've gone super-precise with the quantities to ensure you get the right balance of flavours, and if you make loads of blends and have one set of standard-sized jars, you'll know what you're aiming for and what the yield will be. Having said that, these recipes are easy to scale up or down, so if you want to make a bigger or smaller batch, you can. Sometimes it's fun on a lazy Sunday to just get the tunes on and make a load of blends.

Master spice blends

Notes

*You can buy Szechuan peppercorn powder as well as the whole form, so grab this if you like, as it's much easier.

**Allspice berries can be tricky to get hold of but you can generally find the powder in most supermarkets or online. Make sure when you are buying it that you avoid the common mistake of confusing it with Mixed Spice. They are not the same!

***Rose petals are optional here, but if you have a rose bush at home, the petals are edible (as long as they have not been sprayed with any chemicals!). Give them a wash, dry and grind them up, then freeze in bags. As a family we travelled to Morocco and saw lots of people growing and drying rose petals to add to their ras el hanout blends. Mum's been doing the same ever since.

Baharat
Makes 100g (3½oz)

27g paprika
18g cumin
14g black peppercorns
7g coriander
7g cinnamon
4g nutmeg, grated
1g green cardamom seeds or powder
2g cloves
8g ginger powder
7g chilli powder
8g allspice**

Put any whole spices into the coffee grinder or pestle and mortar. Grind. Then add in any powdered ingredients and mix by hand to combine.

Label and store in a clean jar in a cool, dark place for up to 6 months.

Berbere
Makes 100g (3½oz)

1g green cardamom seeds or green cardamom seed powder
11g ground fenugreek
15g coriander
9g black peppercorns
4g cloves
15g paprika
13g ginger powder
4g cinnamon
4g chilli flakes (red pepper flakes)
5g onion granules
4g garlic granules
13g salt

Put any whole spices into your coffee grinder or pestle and mortar. Grind to your desired consistency. Then add in any powdered ingredients and your chilli flakes, onion and garlic granules and salt. Mix by hand to combine.

Label and store in a clean jar in a cool, dark place for up to 6 months.

Cajun
Makes 100g (3½oz)

27g cumin
27g coriander
27g paprika
7g black peppercorns
7g dried oregano
7g salt

Put any whole spices into the coffee grinder or pestle and mortar. Grind. Then add in any powdered ingredients, the oregano and salt and mix by hand to combine.

Label and store in a clean jar in a cool, dark place for up to 6 months.

Chinese Seven Spice
Makes 100g (3½oz)

19g star anise
13g cinnamon
22g fennel seeds
26g Szechuan pepper
4g cloves
2g white pepper
2g black pepper
13g salt

If you're using Szechuan peppercorns*, grind them with any other whole spices, then mix everything else together by hand to combine.

Label and store in a clean jar in a cool, dark place for up to 6 months.

Garam Masala
Makes 100g (3½oz)

35g cumin
28g coriander
11g black peppercorns
6g ginger powder
3g cloves
8g cinnamon
4g star anise
2g nutmeg, grated
2g cardamom

Put any whole spices into the coffee grinder or pestle and mortar. Grind. Then add in any powdered ingredients and mix by hand to combine.

Label and store in a clean jar in a cool, dark place for up to 6 months.

Gingerbread/ Speculaas
Makes 100g (3½oz)

38g cinnamon
6g nutmeg, grated
6g cloves
26g ginger powder
4g cardamom
6g white pepper
13g allspice**

Add any whole spices into your coffee grinder or pestle and mortar. Grind to your desired consistency. Then add in any powdered ingredients and mix by hand to combine.

Label and store in a clean jar in a cool, dark place for up to 6 months.

Harissa
Makes 100g (3½oz)
Here we have included chilli powder and chilli flakes but if you don't have chilli flakes then double the amount of powder.

21g paprika
3g coriander
3g caraway
3g cumin
27g chilli powder
27g chilli flakes (red pepper flakes)
5g garlic granules
10g salt

Put any whole spices into your coffee grinder or pestle and mortar. Grind to your desired consistency. Then add in any powdered ingredients and your chilli flakes, garlic granules and salt. Mix by hand to combine.

Label and store in a clean jar in a cool, dark place for up to 6 months.

Italian Seasoning
Makes 100g (3½oz)

22g dried basil
22g dried oregano
11g dried rosemary
22g dried parsley
16g dried thyme
4g garlic granules
4g onion granules

No need for blitzing or grinding here, just mix your ingredients together thoroughly by hand in a small bowl.

Label and store in a clean jar in a cool, dark place for up to 6 months.

Jerk
Makes 100g (3½oz)

20g chilli powder
10g dried thyme
6g dried parsley
10g paprika
10g allspice**
5g black peppercorns
5g nutmeg
2g cinnamon
10g sugar
6g onion granules
6g garlic granules
10g salt

Add any whole spices into the coffee grinder or pestle and mortar. Grind. Then add in any powdered ingredients, the dried herbs, sugar, onion and garlic granules and salt and mix by hand to combine.

Label and store in a clean jar in a cool, dark place for up to 6 months.

Mexican (Tex-Mex)
Makes 100g (3½oz)

29g cumin
15g paprika
19g chilli powder
4g dried oregano
15g sugar
4g onion granules
4g garlic granules
10g salt

If you're using cumin seeds, blitz those in your coffee grinder or grind in a pestle and mortar, then mix everything else together by hand to combine.

Label and store in a clean jar in a cool, dark place for up to 6 months.

Ras el Hanout
Makes 100g (3½oz)

2g cloves
3g star anise
5g allspice**
2g cardamom
7g black peppercorns
5g chilli powder
9g cinnamon
9g coriander
9g cumin
9g nutmeg, grated
9g paprika
9g ginger powder
9g turmeric powder
7g sugar
3g dried rose petals (optional)***
7g salt

Put any whole spices into the coffee grinder or pestle and mortar. Grind. Then add in any powdered ingredients, the sugar, rose petals (if using) and salt and mix by hand to combine.

Label and store in a clean jar in a cool, dark place for up to 6 months.

Tandoori Masala
Makes 100g (3½oz)

8g ginger powder
3g turmeric powder
22g coriander
7g chilli powder
8g cumin
10g beetroot powder (optional)
4g fenugreek
5g black peppercorns
3g cinnamon
2g cloves
2g cardamom
4g nutmeg, grated
5g sugar
5g onion granules
5g garlic granules
5g salt

Put any whole spices into the coffee grinder or pestle and mortar. Grind. Then add in any powdered ingredients, the sugar, onion and garlic granules and salt and mix by hand to combine.

Label and store in a clean jar in a cool, dark place for up to 6 months.

Tarka

Makes 100g (3½oz)

50g black mustard
  seeds
50g cumin seeds

This blend uses whole spices; simply mix the seeds together and store in a jar for when you need them. This Tarka blend is great when used to make a flavourful oil and it is used in many of the Indian recipes in this book.

Togarashi

Makes 100g (3½oz)
Togarashi works really well with dried orange peel but as this ingredient is hard to get it's listed as optional here. Don't stress if you can't get it; your blend will still be lovely.

8g Szechuan pepper
8g ginger powder
12g seaweed powder
26g chilli flakes (red
  pepper flakes)
17g white sesame
  seeds
17g black sesame
  seeds
12g ground dried
  orange peel
  (optional)

If you're using Szechuan peppercorns*, grind them with the ginger and seaweed, then mix everything else together by hand to combine.

Label and store in a clean jar in a cool, dark place for up to 6 months.

Sri Lankan Curry Powder

Makes 100g (3½oz)

If you've managed to get yourself some curry leaves, then they are amazing in this recipe, but don't worry if you can't buy any, your blend is still going to pack a flavourful punch.

20g coriander
22g cumin
28g fennel seeds
6g fenugreek
4g cloves
3g cardamom
12g chilli powder
6g cinnamon
Handful of dried curry
  leaves (optional)

Add any whole spices and curry leaves (if using) into the coffee grinder or pestle and mortar. Grind. Then add in any powdered ingredients and mix by hand to combine.

Label and store in a clean jar in a cool, dark place for up to 6 months.

Za'atar

Makes 100g (3½oz)

37g sesame seeds
37g sumac
9g dried thyme
5g dried marjoram
5g dried oregano
7g salt

So simple: mix all your ingredients by hand to combine in a bowl.

Label and store in a clean jar in a cool, dark place for up to 6 months.

A (quick) word on chillies

Most of us have had the experience of cooking a fantastic meal, only to have it ruined by too much heat. I can't promise miracles, but hopefully this short introduction will help you have less of those heated moments.

Usually, in any chilli-lover's family, there will be someone who is not so keen on the heat, or there might be a child who is not yet old enough to enjoy the heat. Either way, we all know someone who does not like their food quite so hot or simply does not like chilli heat full stop! I must confess that when someone says they don't like chillies, I see that as a challenge, and I have successfully converted a few haters into believers. But that's not always going to cut it. Knowing a little about chillies, what to look for and what parts of the fruit to use, will make you feel more confident in using them in your kitchen.

A warm welcome to the chilli

Chillies - in all their forms - add flavour, balance and depth to your dishes but they need to be used with awareness and care. Fresh chillies have a different flavour profile to dried: they add a fruity, citrus flavour to dishes, whereas dried lend a more rounded, earthy flavour.

The most common chillies used by the home cook are different varieties of *Capsicum annuum*. You will likely know these as 'cayenne' chillies, whether they are a bird's eye or Thai chilli, a green finger chilli or a jalapeño.

Green chillies are milder than red as they are not fully ripe. Fully ripe red chillies are hotter and sweeter. A quick rule of thumb is that the smaller the chilli, the hotter it will be.

Try to use green finger chillies in Indian dishes, as you won't get the right taste otherwise. Similarly, use the more rounded jalapeños in North and South American cooking.

However, please be aware that this guide does not work with Scotch Bonnet or habanero chillies, which need careful handling as they are super-hot.

If you're a fan of fiery dishes, do give them a go, but if you prefer your dishes milder, avoid any fresh or dried varieties, as well as pickles or sauces that contain either of these.

Two tricks to control the heat of fresh chillies

Here are some super-simple tricks that will help you to have fewer chilli disasters when cooking:

- **Remove the source of the heat**
The source of the heat is the white membrane, which you see when you slice into a chilli. The seeds are attached to this membrane, so removing it together with the seeds will significantly reduce the heat. This is such an easy lesson and something you'll never forget once you've been told.

- **Prick the chilli with a pin or a knife**
Another way to control chilli heat is to use your chillies whole. You literally just prick the bottom of the chilli with a pin, or nick it with a knife, and pop it into your dish. It will release some flavour and heat into the dish, but not all. You can easily remove it at the end of the cooking time and taste your dish to see if it requires more heat; if so, just chop the chilli and add it back into the dish until you achieve the desired heat level. When using whole dried chillies, you can take the same approach: leaving them intact during cooking and testing the recipe carefully chopping them up and adding them back in if desired.

Go easy

At the end of the day, like any other ingredient, it's all about getting the right balance and creating the sort of spice level that you love; that is what delicious food is all about. Find the heat level that works for you by starting with a small amount and adding bit by bit, tasting regularly along the way.

Less is more when using our harissa blend, ground chilli or chilli flakes (red pepper flakes). It's easy to overpower a dish, so it is better to go softly, taste as you go and add more if needed.

Simple Lunches

I refuse to miss out on the opportunity for an incredible lunch and I hope I can convince you of the same! Life is busy: running a business through the week and having a young family can sometimes be chaos, but I always find time to stop and enjoy a tasty midday treat. In the office, we always gather round the table and eat together, as it gives us that all-important social time. This is not the occasion for fancy presentation or long and slow marinades: the recipes in this section are so quick to make, many of them taking as little as 10 minutes to throw together.

Spiced Peach and Goat's Cheese Salad

2 peaches
2 tsp honey
2 tsp Italian Seasoning (page 26)
1 tsp olive oil
1 tsp water

Salad
½ cucumber, you can peel if you don't
   like the skin
2 tsp white wine vinegar
Sea salt
150g (5½oz) cherry tomatoes
15g (½oz) basil leaves
15g (½oz) parsley leaves
50g (1¾oz) crumbly goat's cheese
1 tbsp olive oil
4 tbsp Chimichurri (page 199), to serve

This is bright, fresh and gorgeous in summer. Make sure your peaches aren't overripe or too soft, or they'll fall apart in the pan. In fact, this is a great way to liven up a couple of too-hard supermarket peaches.

Ribbon the cucumber with a swivel-head vegetable peeler, stopping before you reach the seeds. Put in a bowl with the white wine vinegar and a pinch of salt, then toss to combine. Set aside.

Halve the peaches and pull out the stones. Whisk together the honey, Italian seasoning, olive oil and water.

Heat a frying pan (skillet) over a moderate heat, dip each peach half into the spiced honey, and cook for 3 minutes, until starting to colour. Spoon some more of the honey over each peach half, then flip and cook until well caramelized. Spoon the rest of the honey over the top, flip once more, and cook until well browned. Take the pan off the heat and set aside.

Slice the tomatoes into halves or quarters. Squeeze the cucumber then toss with the tomatoes, and the herbs. Dot with the goat's cheese, top with the peaches and dress with the tablespoon of olive oil before serving.

Serve with the lovely fresh chimichurri drizzled over.

Pimped-up Scrambled Eggs

If you usually like your scrambled eggs soft and creamy, then you'll feel like you're overcooking these. Don't be tempted to take them off too early; they need the extra time in the pan for the spice blend to be at its best. Eat them piled on buttered toast.

Serves 2

5 eggs
1 tsp Sri Lankan Curry Powder (page 28)
Butter

To serve
4 slices white bread, toasted and buttered
2 spring onions (scallions), ends removed and finely chopped
Fresh coriander (cilantro), roughly chopped (optional)

Crack the eggs into a bowl and add the Sri Lankan curry powder. Beat with a fork until no visible streaks of yolk or white remain.

Melt a knob of butter in a non-stick frying pan (skillet) and tip in the eggs. Cook over a gentle heat, stirring occasionally at first then constantly as the eggs cook. Once the eggs are starting to clump, pull the cooked egg into the centre of the pan and allow any uncooked egg to fill in the space.

Once the eggs are cooked, scoop them out of the pan; you want them completely cooked but not dried out.

Serve spooned over your favourite toasted white bread spread with oodles of butter. Scatter over the spring onion, and fresh coriander, if using.

Halloumi Wraps with Baharat and Pomegranate Seeds

On page 190, we recommend making your own flatbreads, but for a 10-minute lunch simply grab what's in your cupboard and pile on the flavour! The pomegranate seeds give a lovely pop of flavour and balance the earthiness of the baharat, and the chutney is going to elevate this quick lunch to a real midday treat.

Serves 2

2 tbsp olive oil
1 heaped tsp Baharat (page 25)
1 block of halloumi (250g/9oz)
2 flatbreads

To serve
Crispy salad leaves
1 tbsp pomegranate seeds
2 tsp Zingy Mint and Coriander Chutney (page 198)

Mix the olive oil and baharat in a large bowl.

Chop the halloumi into 2cm (¾in) strips and add to the bowl, stir to combine.

Heat a heavy-bottomed frying pan (skillet) over a medium heat. Add your halloumi with the oil and spices and cook for about 1-2 minutes on each side.

Heat your flatbreads in a separate pan according to the packet instructions.

Arrange your halloumi on top of the flatbreads and pile on the salad leaves, pomegranate seeds and chutney.

Quick Shakshuka

When I was 18, I embarked on my first round-the-world travel trip, and had little awareness of the incredible international foodie delights awaiting me. Travelling alone, I often bumped into other solo travellers and then travelled with them. I first tasted shakshuka on this trip in a hostel in Costa Rica, where it was made by an incredible Israeli couple I met. It blew my mind, as I had never eaten eggs this way and never for breakfast!

Shakshuka means 'a mixture' in Arabic, but it is potentially from an old Berber word meaning a ragout (stew). It is the perfect combination of vegetables, tomatoes, eggs and spices, cooked in a way that brings them all together in one pan.

Heat a large frying pan (skillet) over a medium heat. Add the oil and, once hot, fry the tarka for 20 seconds, taking care not to burn the spices. Quickly add the onion and chorizo, and cook, stirring regularly for about 8-10 minutes, or until they have softened and slightly coloured.

Next, add the garlic and red pepper and continue to cook for a further 5 minutes. Add the tomatoes, sugar and tomato purée to the pan and cook for several minutes until nicely blended. Add the harissa blend and season with the salt and pepper.

Make some wells in the mixture with the back of a spoon. Crack in the eggs, one at a time, directly over the pan. Try to aim the eggs into the wells but don't worry if the whites aren't perfectly inside them. Placing the eggs evenly around the rim and one in the centre can look lovely. Cover the pan with a lid. Allow everything to simmer for 10 minutes, or until the eggs are cooked and the sauce has slightly reduced.

Meanwhile, make your ciabatta toast.

After the 10 minutes are up and the eggs are cooked to your liking, turn off the heat. Gently lift the lid, check for seasoning and add a little more salt and pepper if needed.

Serve with the crusty ciabatta and the parsley and coriander scattered on top.

1 tbsp olive oil
1 tsp Tarka (page 28)
1 onion, peeled and finely diced
60g (2¼oz) chorizo, sliced into rounds
1 garlic clove, minced
1 red (bell) pepper, diced
2 x 400g (14oz) cans chopped tomatoes, or 800g (1lb 12oz) Big Batch Tomato Sauce (page 187) if you have some made
1 tbsp sugar
2 tbsp tomato purée (paste)
½ tbsp Harissa (page 26)
½ tsp sea salt
Freshly ground black pepper, to taste
6 eggs

To serve
Freshly cut ciabatta bread, lightly toasted and buttered
2 tbsp roughly chopped fresh parsley
2 tbsp roughly chopped coriander (cilantro)

Serves 4–6, depending on your appetite

Spiced Frittata with a Leafy Salad

Ready to experiment with your blends? This recipe is equally amazing with: Za'atar, Jerk, Tandoori, Harissa

I make this all the time with any potatoes left in the fridge after the weekend. It's also a great lunch for the team at Spice Kitchen when we've got a busy day, because it serves a few and is really quick to throw together.

Serves 4

300g (10½oz) baby new potatoes
1 tbsp vegetable, sunflower or rapeseed (canola) oil
1 tbsp Tandoori Masala (page 27)
100g (3½oz) kale (hard stalks removed) and chopped
100g (3½oz) frozen peas
6 eggs
100ml (scant ½ cup) double (heavy) cream
Generous pinch of salt
1 tbsp chopped chives

Salad
3 tbsp Greek-style yoghurt
1 tbsp olive oil
2 tsp lemon juice
2 tsp Tandoori Masala (page 27)
200g (7oz) mixed salad leaves or rocket (arugula)

Heat your oven to 180°C fan/200°C/400°F/gas mark 6.

Scrub the potatoes, add to a small saucepan and cover with cold water. Bring to the boil, then turn down to simmer for 10 minutes, until the potatoes can be pierced with a fork. Drain and set aside to cool a little.

Slice the potatoes in half or in thirds. Warm the oil in a frying pan (skillet), ideally one that can go in the oven, add the potatoes and sprinkle over the spice mix. Cook for a couple of minutes until everything smells gorgeously fragrant, then add the kale.

Continue to cook until the potatoes are crisp and golden at their edges and the kale is crisp but still vibrant green. Stir through the peas, then remove from the heat. If you don't have an ovenproof frying pan you can tip the vegetables into a baking dish once they're cooked.

Beat the eggs with the cream, season with salt, and add the chives. Pour over the vegetables and transfer to the oven.

Cook for 8 minutes until puffed and brown. Meanwhile, whisk together the yoghurt, olive oil, lemon juice and tandoori blend. Taste for seasoning.

Wash and dry the salad leaves if needed, then toss through the dressing. Serve the frittata hot, in large slices, with the salad.

Homemade Pot Noodle

I LOVE a pot noodle. It's such a great lunch for super-busy days. This is one you can prepare at home and take to the office. It's packed full of veggies so it's nutritious and will hopefully keep you going until teatime.

All you need to do is prepare all your solid ingredients, throw them into a bowl in the morning, cover with beeswax wraps or cling film (plastic wrap) and take to work. Then, when your belly is growling at lunchtime, add the boiling water and wait for the magic to happen.

Serves 1

300ml (1¼ cups) water
40g (1½oz) noodles (rice, spinach or egg, depending on your preference)
1 tbsp Togarashi (page 28)
1 tbsp miso paste
1 tbsp soy sauce
1cm (½in) red or green chilli, minced
1 tsp grated fresh ginger
25g (1oz) sweetcorn or peas, whichever you prefer
5cm (2in) carrot, shaved into ribbons
½ spring onion (scallion), finely sliced
Zest and juice of 1 lime
25g (1oz) spinach leaves, chopped

Boil the measured water in a kettle.

Put your noodles to the bottom of the jar (or bowl) and then top with the rest of the ingredients. Gently pour the boiling water over your ingredients so that they are covered. Cover with foil or the lid from your jar and leave for 10 minutes. If you have access to a microwave you can always speed up the process and cook on full power for 2 minutes (just be sure to remove the lid from the jar if it's metal!).

Cajun-style Potato and Chorizo Hash

A fantastic leftovers brunch. If you have boiled or roast potatoes in the fridge, they're great here. Otherwise, chop some waxy potatoes into chunks, cover them with cold water and bring them to a simmer. Cook until you can insert a knife into one without resistance, then drain.

Serves 3–4

2 tbsp vegetable, sunflower or rapeseed (canola) oil
1 large onion, peeled and sliced into rounds
1 tbsp Cajun blend (page 25)
225g (8oz) chorizo, crumbled or sliced into rounds
500g (1lb 2oz) leftover cooked potatoes, chopped into chunks
2 garlic cloves, very finely sliced
3 sprigs fresh rosemary

To serve
1 egg per person
Sprouting broccoli
1 tbsp per person of Harissa Kraut (page 200)

Heat the oil in a large frying pan (skillet) over a moderate heat. Add the onion and cook for 10 minutes, stirring regularly, until soft and golden. Add the Cajun blend and stir through. Cook for a couple of minutes, then add the chorizo.

Stir the chorizo through the onions and cook for a couple of minutes until starting to colour. Add the potatoes and occasionally stir very gently, letting them crisp in the fat in the pan. Cook for 8 minutes. Stir through the garlic and rosemary and cook for a final couple of minutes.

Meanwhile, soft boil the eggs (lower them into boiling water for 6 minutes, then plunge into cold water and peel), lightly steam some broccoli, and plate up with a spoonful of harissa kraut on the side of the hash.

43

Sprouts with Egg Noodles and Togarashi

This is a great working lunch or easy dinner for one – it takes no more than 10 minutes from start to finish. The sauce is delicious made with tahini or with peanut butter, but it's particularly great with darker Chinese sesame paste, which you can find in Asian supermarkets.

Serves 1

100g (3½oz) Brussels sprouts
1 tbsp sesame oil, for frying
1 nest egg noodles

Sauce
1 tbsp Chinese sesame paste
2 tsp dark soy sauce
1 tsp rice vinegar
1 tsp sesame oil
1 tbsp Togarashi (page 28)

To serve
3 tbsp fried onions

Trim the stem and any ageing outer leaves from each sprout and cut into quarters. Heat the sesame oil in a frying pan (skillet) or wok and fry the sprouts until they start to crisp and colour.

Meanwhile, bring a small saucepan of water to the boil and cook the egg noodles following the packet instructions. Drain, then rinse under cold water.

Whisk together the sesame paste, soy sauce, rice vinegar, sesame oil and togarashi. Add the drained noodles to the sprouts and stir the sauce through. Serve with plenty of crispy fried onions for crunch and texture.

Mushrooms on Toast

I love mushrooms. It's fair to say I'm obsessed with them. I wanted to include a whole section in this book and dedicate it just to mushrooms. But I applied some self-control and instead offer you this lovely mushroom lunch recipe. I make it all the time and my guess is that once you've tried it, so will you.

Serves 1 (don't share!), but easy to scale up

Knob of butter
1 tsp vegetable, sunflower or rapeseed (canola) oil
125g (4½oz) portobello or chestnut mushrooms, sliced
2 tsp Za'atar (page 28)
Pinch of salt
1 slice of your favourite bread
2 tbsp ricotta
Fresh parsley, roughly chopped

Melt the butter and oil together in a large frying pan (skillet) over a moderate heat (the oil prevents the butter from burning - mushrooms take a little while to cook). Add the mushrooms to the pan. Make sure they have space in the pan - you want them to brown, not sweat!

Stir frequently and, once the mushrooms have started to brown, add the za'atar blend and cook for a further 5 minutes. Taste and season with salt.

Push the mushrooms to the side and fry your bread on both sides until crisp. Spread with ricotta, top with the mushrooms and some chopped parsley, and serve.

Quick Tomato, Onion and Herb Tart

1 tbsp vegetable, sunflower or
rapeseed (canola) oil
3 red onions, sliced into half moons
1 tsp caster (superfine) sugar
Pinch of salt
1 tbsp Italian Seasoning (page 26)
2 tsp balsamic vinegar
1 sheet ready-rolled puff pastry
500g (1lb 2oz) cherry tomatoes
150g (5½oz) pitted black olives
1 egg (skip the egg wash if you're
vegan, or use a splash of oat
milk instead)
Handful of chopped fresh parsley
Zest of 1 unwaxed lemon

A sheet of ready-rolled puff pastry makes this a really simple lunch, and although cooking the onions needs your attention, everything else is incredibly low effort. Make sure you cook the pastry until it's deep, burnished golden-brown; too pallid and it will still be soft and floppy underneath.

Warm the vegetable oil in a frying pan (skillet) and fry the onions over a moderate heat, stirring frequently so that they soften but don't stick. After 5 minutes, add the sugar and salt. After another 5 minutes, add the Italian seasoning and the vinegar and cook for a final 5 minutes. Set aside to cool.

Preheat the oven to 190°C fan/210°C/410°F/gas mark 6½. Unroll the puff pastry sheet onto a lined baking tray (sheet) and create a border by using a knife to score a line a little way in from the edge (don't slice all the way through the pastry).

Spread the onions over the pastry inside the border, then top with the tomatoes and olives. Beat the egg and paint it over the border. Transfer the tart to the oven and bake for 20 minutes until risen and a rich golden-brown around the edges.

Top with the parsley and lemon zest and serve while warm.

Sanjay's Ultimate Stir-fry

I was taught this recipe by my friend Pete who spent three years living and working in China after we left university. I still make it to this day, although I vary up the veggies depending on what's in my fridge or freezer. For instance, if you don't have pak choi (bok choy), you can use cabbage and it will be just as gorgeous.

2 chicken breasts, sliced
2 tbsp dark soy sauce
1 tbsp minced garlic
1 tbsp Chinese Seven Spice (page 25)
1 tbsp rice wine vinegar
Pinch of sugar
1 tsp cornflour (cornstarch)
2 tbsp vegetable, sunflower or
    rapeseed (canola) oil
1 small onion, finely sliced
2 spring onions (scallions), sliced
½ green chilli, minced
1 thumb-sized piece of ginger,
    cut into matchsticks
100g (3½oz) mushrooms, sliced
1 red (bell) pepper, deseeded
    and sliced
150g (5½oz) broccoli, broken into
    bite-sized florets
150g (5½oz) cauliflower, broken into
    bite-sized florets
2 pak choi (bok choy), ends removed
    and leaves separated

To serve
2 nests egg or rice noodles
1 tbsp sesame seeds (optional)

In a large bowl, mix the sliced chicken with the soy sauce, garlic, Chinese seven spice, rice wine, sugar and cornflour.

Heat the sunflower oil in a wok over a high heat. When hot, carefully add the onion and let sizzle for about a minute.

Add the chicken and stir-fry over a high heat until the meat is browned. Add the spring onions, green chilli and ginger and continue to cook for a further 3-5 minutes, stirring regularly.

Now add the mushrooms, red pepper, broccoli and cauliflower and continue to stir-fry for a further 3 minutes. You can also add an extra splash of soy sauce at this stage, if you like.

Now is the time to prepare your noodles. Cook following the packet instructions and drain.

Meanwhile add the pak choi (bok choy) to the wok and cook until slightly wilted.

Scatter over the sesame seeds (if using) and serve your stir-fry spooned over the noodles.

Spiced Falafel and Hummus Wrap

I became a falafel addict while living on Birmingham's so-called Curry Mile during my uni days. They were cheap, filling and so, so tasty. Although the list of ingredients looks long, you could make a simpler version, by buying a pot of hummus instead and stirring your spice blend through it!

First, make the falafel mix. Drain the defrosted peas and chickpeas really well (too wet and the falafel will fall apart). Put the peas, chickpeas, baharat, flour, baking powder, garlic, tahini and salt in a food processor and blitz to a coarse mixture.

Form the falafel mix into about 18 balls, squashing them together really well. Refrigerate for at least an hour, or pop in the freezer until solid.

Make the hummus following the method on page 193, adding the za'atar when you blitz all the ingredients. Once combined, add 3 tablespoons of cold water and blitz until smooth. Taste and season with salt and set aside.

Preheat the oven to 180°C fan/200°C/400°F/gas mark 6. Dip each falafel in olive oil and place on a lined baking sheet. Bake for 30 minutes, turning them over halfway through.

Peel and grate the carrots, then toss through the vinegar with a pinch of salt. Squeeze well. Finely shred the lettuce.

To assemble, warm the flatbreads for a couple of minutes in the oven (switched off) once the falafel are cooked and cooling. Spread each with a generous amount of hummus and three falafel. Top with some lettuce, carrot and a couple of pickled chillies if you wish. Wrap and serve.

Serves 6

Falafel
200g (7oz) frozen peas, defrosted
1 x 400g (14oz) can of chickpeas (garbanzo beans), rinsed and drained
2 tbsp Baharat (page 25)
4 tbsp plain (all-purpose) flour
1 tsp baking powder
2 garlic cloves
1 tbsp tahini
Pinch of salt
Olive oil, for baking

Hummus
1 x quantity Homemade Hummus (page 193)
1 heaped tsp Za'atar (page 28)

To serve
½ head Iceberg lettuce
2 carrots
1 tsp cider vinegar
6 large flatbreads
Pickled green chillies (optional)

Mumbai Grilled Sandwich

Serves 1

The Mumbai sandwich is an iconic street food from India and just the thing when you want a hot lunch but don't have much time. Hot and buttery with oozy cheese, this is the stuff of dreams.

1 tsp butter, for spreading
2 slices of sourdough
1 tsp Zingy Mint and Coriander Chutney (page 198), plus extra to serve
1 potato, peeled, boiled and left to cool, sliced
½ tomato, sliced
¼ small red onion, peeled and finely sliced
2.5cm (1in) chunk of cucumber, peeled and sliced
50–60g (about 2oz) mature Cheddar cheese, grated
1 tsp Garam Masala (page 26)
Salt and freshly ground black pepper
1 tsp Spiced Tomato Chutney (page 196), to serve

Butter your bread on both sides. Spread the zingy mint and coriander chutney on one slice, then layer on the potato, tomato, onion, cucumber and grated cheese. Sprinkle over the garam masala and season to taste.

Set a griddle pan over a medium heat and allow to heat for 3 minutes. This will allow it to get nice and hot before you add your sandwich. While it's heating, top your sandwich with the second bread slice, then toast in your pan for a few minutes on each side, until golden and beautifully crispy.

Serve with tomato chutney and some more coriander chutney on the side.

Tofu with Rice and Pickles

If you've not tried togarashi before, this is a great place to start. It's delicious alongside tofu and sweet, sticky rice. You can add any sort of pickles you fancy, so if you've got a jar of something you love in your fridge, use it. But radish and cucumber are ideal for a quick pickle that will be ready in the time it takes you to cook the rice! You can use the Perfectly Fluffy Rice recipe on page 189, if you prefer. This rice is stickier and sweeter (thanks to the mirin), but you'll know what you like best!

Rice
100g (3½oz) sushi rice
1 tbsp mirin
Pinch of salt

Pickles
½ cucumber
6 radishes
3 tbsp rice vinegar
½ tsp salt
½ tsp caster (superfine) sugar
½ tsp togarashi (page 28)

Tofu
2 tbsp dark soy sauce
1 tbsp mirin
280g (10oz) firm tofu, cut into 0.5cm (¼in) slices
Vegetable, sunflower or rapeseed (canola) oil, for shallow frying
3 tbsp cornflour (cornstarch)
1 tsp togarashi, or less, depending on your chilli heat preference (page 28)

Rinse the rice three times, until the water is running clear. Drain well, then put the rice in a lidded saucepan with 125ml (½ cup) water and leave to soak for 5 minutes while you make the pickle.

Meanwhile, slice the cucumber and radishes very finely, on the diagonal, and place in a bowl. Bring the rest of the pickle ingredients to a simmer in a small saucepan, then pour over the cucumber and radish slices. Leave to pickle while you prepare everything else.

Put a lid on the saucepan with the rice and bring to the boil. Turn down immediately and slow simmer for 10 minutes, with the lid on, until the water is no longer higher than the level of the rice. Try not to lift the lid too frequently to check it; you don't want the steam to escape. Set the rice aside, with the lid clamped tightly on, and allow it to steam for 10 minutes. Once it has steamed, stir the rice with a fork and mix the mirin and salt through.

To marinate the tofu slices, mix together the soy sauce and mirin in a shallow bowl and lay the tofu in the marinade for 5 minutes, turning once.

Heat a thin layer of vegetable oil (less than 1cm/½in) in a frying pan (skillet) or wide saucepan. Tip the cornflour into a bowl. Shake each slice of tofu and press each side into the cornflour. Lower carefully into the oil and cook the slices until crisp and golden on each side. Drain on paper towels and, while still hot, season with togarashi.

Serve the tofu on top of the rice, with the pickles alongside.

Za'atar King Prawns with Garlic Yoghurt

Succulent prawns, spiced and grilled to perfection, are one of my favourite reasons for being alive! Cook this beauty for a quick lunch and be happy for the rest of the day. For a twist on this recipe, you can swap out the za'atar and use the harissa or tandoori blend instead.

You will need 4-6 metal skewer sor bamboo skewers soaked in water.

Mix together the olive oil, lemon zest and half the juice, the ginger-garlic paste, salt and za'atar in a bowl. Add the prawns and combine to coat evenly. Leave to marinate for around 30 minutes.

Preheat your grill (broiler) to medium-high heat, making sure you oil the grill before adding the prawns so they cook well and don't stick.

Skewer the prawns, place on the grill and cook for 3 minutes on each side.

Squeeze over the remaining lemon juice and serve the prawns immediately with the yoghurt on the side, a crisp salad and a big hunk of buttered bread.

3 tbsp olive oil
Zest of 1 and juice of 2 unwaxed
  lemons
1 tbsp Ginger-Garlic Paste (page 190)
1 tsp salt
½ tsp Za'atar (page 28)
700g (1lb 9oz) king prawns (jumbo
  shrimp), peeled, deveined and tails
  left on

To serve
2 tbsp Garlic Yoghurt (page 193)
Crispy salad leaves
Freshly cut and buttered bread

Serves 2

Midweek Dinners

I often wonder if 'What's for dinner?' is the most asked question in the universe! Our world has changed to the point where, for many of us, a midweek meal is something we are prepared to dedicate 30 minutes to, or an hour at best. We simply don't have the time in an evening to do justice to this meal. But worry not, the recipes in this chapter will enable you to create a massively flavoursome meal in no time at all.

Coriander and Tandoori Fishcakes

A chippy tea of sorts: beautiful fish, potatoes, peas, tartare sauce. These fishcakes are great with cod, but they'll also work with your favourite fish: haddock, salmon or mackerel are all lovely. Serve them alongside a well-dressed pile of watercress in the summer or some steamed greens in the colder months.

Peel the potatoes and chop them into similar-sized pieces. Put in a saucepan, cover with cold water, set over a high heat and bring to the boil. Reduce to a simmer and cook until a knife can be inserted easily into the potatoes.

Meanwhile, put the cod in a separate lidded pan with the peppercorns and halved onion. Cover with cold water, bring to the boil then turn the heat off and put the lid on. Leave to cool until you can comfortably touch the side of the pan.

Drain the potatoes and mash well. Fold through the chopped coriander, the tandoori masala and a decent pinch of salt. Gently flake the cod and fold it through the mash (you want the flakes to be generous, so don't fold too vigorously).

Shape the potato mixture into four fish cakes then place in the fridge for 30 minutes to firm up.

Meanwhile, make the tartare sauce following the instructions on page 195, cover and leave in the fridge until you're ready to serve.

Warm the oil in a wide frying pan (skillet). Lightly coat each fishcake in flour, shaking off the excess, and fry until golden brown - about 6 minutes on each side. Make sure you flip gently, so they don't fall apart!

Serve with the tartare sauce, your choice of watercress or steamed greens and a squeeze of lemon juice over the fishcakes.

450g (1lb) floury potatoes for mashing
300g (10½oz) cod fillets
1 tsp whole black peppercorns
1 onion, peeled and halved
20g (¾oz) chopped coriander (cilantro)
1 tsp Tandoori Masala (page 27)
Salt, to taste
2 tbsp vegetable, sunflower or rapeseed (canola) oil
50g (1¾oz) plain (all-purpose) flour

To serve
Tartare Sauce with a Twist (page 195)
Watercress or steamed greens
A squeeze of lemon juice

Makes 4 fishcakes

Matar Paneer

This dish is perfect for a quick midweek meal. Growing up, it was an absolute staple in our home every couple of weeks and I still love it to this day. For serving midweek, it's nice to keep the sauce light, but if you fancy a treat, you can make it more indulgent by adding cream. We love to drizzle it with a Tarka-infused oil once everything is cooked.

Serves 2

3 tbsp vegetable, sunflower or rapeseed (canola) oil
½ onion, finely diced
2 tsp Ginger-Garlic Paste (page 190)
1 green chilli, minced
2 tsp Garam Masala (page 26)
4 tbsp passata (strained tomatoes)
½ tsp turmeric (optional but really tasty if you have it)
250ml (generous 1 cup) water
1 tsp salt
200g (7oz) peas
4 cubes frozen spinach
200g (7oz) paneer, cut into 2cm (¾in) cubes
½ tsp Tarka (page 28)
1 tsp roughly chopped coriander (cilantro)

Set a heavy-bottomed frying pan (skillet) over a medium-high heat and add 2 tablespoons of the oil. Once hot, add the onion and cook for about 5 minutes.

Next, stir in the ginger-garlic paste and green chilli. Cook for 1 minute, then add the garam masala, passata, turmeric if using, water and salt. Stir again and continue to cook until the sauce begins to bubble, then turn off the heat. Leave to cool a little and, using a stick blender, blend the mixture until it forms a smooth paste.

Turn the heat back on and bring your sauce to a simmer. Add the peas and spinach and cook for 5 minutes until they have softened, then add the paneer and cook for a further 2-3 minutes.

While your paneer cooks, pour the remaining oil into a smaller frying pan set over a medium-high heat. Once hot, add your tarka and let the whole spices sizzle for around 30 seconds, being careful not to burn.

Ladle the matar paneer into bowls and gently spoon the hot tarka-infused oil over your dish.

Garnish with fresh coriander and serve with rice, naan, chapatis or pitta.

Sweet Potato Bean Burger with Harissa Mayo

Serves 4

400g (14oz) sweet potato, peeled and chopped into chunks
400g (14oz) can of black beans
Large pinch of salt
2 tsp Harissa (page 26)
20g coriander (cilantro), chopped
50g (1¾oz) porridge oats (rolled oats)
40g (1½oz) cornflour (cornstarch)
Vegetable, sunflower or rapeseed (canola) oil, for shallow frying

To serve
4 burger buns – ones with a decent crust are best here
100g (3½oz) Harissa Mayo (page 193)
Iceberg lettuce, shredded

If you have some sweet potatoes and a can of black beans then you are all set for an amazing burger experience! The sweetness of the potatoes is perfectly balanced by the heady heat of the spiced mayo.

Put the sweet potato into a saucepan, cover with cold water and bring to the boil. As soon as the potato is cooked enough for you to be able to easily insert a fork into a chunk, drain and then return to the hot pan to dry out.

Mash the sweet potato and black beans in a bowl and stir through the rest of the ingredients except for the oil: the mixture should be sticky, but not wet. Line a baking sheet or plate with baking paper and shape the burger mixture into four patties; I spoon the filling into a biscuit (cookie) cutter and press it down firmly so that the patties are nice and tall, but you could also shape them with your hands. Transfer to the fridge for at least 30 minutes.

Pour oil into a non-stick frying pan (skillet) to a depth of 1cm (½in). Heat until hot and gently lower in the burgers. Fry for about 7 minutes on each side or until they're a rich brown. Handle them gently as you flip, as they're a bit delicate. Once crisp on both sides, drain on paper towels.

To assemble the burger, spread the base of the buns with harissa mayo and top with shredded iceberg lettuce. Add the burger, another spoonful of mayo, and the top of the bun. Serve immediately.

Quick Tarka Dal

Midweek cooking doesn't get any easier than this. It's a great option for people on a plant-based diet, or anyone looking for a meat-free option. We have this dish at least once a week, because: it's so quick to throw together with the pre-made Tarka Sauce. My 4-year-old daughter Zara loves it and actually asks for it – it's healthy and SO tasty.

Serves 3–4

160g (5¾oz) red lentils, rinsed 3 or 4 times in cold water
480ml (2 cups) water
½ tsp salt
300ml (1¼ cups) Tarka Sauce (page 188)
100g (3½oz) fresh spinach (optional)

To serve
3 tbsp freshly chopped coriander (cilantro)
½ green chilli, minced (optional)

Add the lentils to a large saucepan and cover with the measured water. Make sure there is about 5cm (2in) of water above the lentils. Add the salt, bring to the boil and then turn down to a simmer. Cover and cook for 5-12 minutes, depending on how much bite you like. As a rough guide, 5 minutes will give you a tender yet firm consistency, whereas after 12 minutes the lentils will begin to break down and become very soft and mushy. Most, if not all, of the water will be absorbed by the lentils.

Once your lentils are cooked, add in the prepared tarka sauce. Stir to combine and allow to heat thoroughly. Simmer for about 5 minutes. You can also add the spinach at this stage, if using. Add a little water if the sauce is too thick (the fresh spinach may release some water). Ladle into bowls. Top with the freshly chopped coriander and green chillies, if using. Serve with rice, salad, naan bread or chapati for a warming midweek treat.

Mamma Spice's Famous Chickpea Curry

I mentioned in the introduction that Mum is famous for her chickpea curry. Follow this recipe and soon you will be too! By using canned chickpeas and the pre-made Tarka Sauce, you're well on your way to a super-quick and incredibly tasty midweek meal.

Serves 2–3

400g (14oz) can chickpeas (garbanzo beans), drained and rinsed
400ml (14fl oz) Tarka Sauce (page 188)
Fresh coriander (cilantro), roughly chopped
1 tbsp Zingy Mint and Coriander Chutney (page 198)
2 tbsp Greek-style yoghurt (optional)

Add the chickpeas and tarka sauce to a saucepan and simmer for 15 minutes on a low-medium heat, stirring regularly, adding a little more water if the curry has thickened too much.

Top with fresh coriander and serve with the zingy chutney, and yoghurt if you wish, with rice, naan, or chapati on the side.

65

Our Pancake Day

This is the one thing we cook in our house more than any other! When we were kids, Mum would make a big batch of pancake batter and have a couple of fillings on the go – a samosa one we had with Spiced Tomato Chutney (page 196), spiced stewed apple, and a big jar of Nutella. I've adopted it at home too and cook it for my daughter Zara, who loves it! We call it 'Our Pancake Day'.

First make the savoury filling. Warm the vegetable oil in a large frying pan (skillet) and fry the onions until just starting to soften. Add the potatoes and keep everything moving. Stir in the tandoori blend and continue to cook until the onions are soft and the potatoes are tender. Set aside and stir in the peas; they will cook in the residual heat. Taste and season with salt.

To make the sweet filling, melt the butter in a small saucepan and add the apples, along with 2 tablespoons of water. Cook until the apples start to collapse, then add the gingerbread blend and sugar. Keep cooking over a low heat, stirring occasionally so that it doesn't stick, until the apples have collapsed entirely into a sauce. Remove from the heat and cover the pan.

For the pancakes, beat the eggs with a couple of tablespoons of the flour until you have a smooth mixture (this will help prevent lumps in your batter). Stir in a splash of milk then a spoonful of flour alternately until you've used both up and the batter has the consistency of single (light) cream. Season with the salt then whisk in the melted butter.

Melt the additional butter in a non-stick frying pan. The melted butter in the batter means you don't have to re-grease between each pancake (and that you don't end up with burnt butter in your frying pan), but a little to start helps the tricky first pancake on its way. Pour about 2 tablespoons of the batter into the centre of your pan and swirl it so it covers the base in a thin layer. Cook until the pancake is light brown in patches underneath, then flip with a spatula (or flip in the air if you're good at that sort of thing).

Distribute the pancakes as you cook them, adding whichever filling each member of the family prefers, or keep the pancakes warm stacked on an ovenproof plate in a very low oven until you're ready to eat and serve with the fillings at the table.

Savoury filling

1 tbsp vegetable, sunflower or rapeseed (canola) oil
2 onions, sliced into half moons
300g (10½oz) potatoes, peeled and diced into pea-sized cubes
2 tsp Tandoori Masala (page 27)
150g (5½oz) frozen peas
Pinch of salt

Sweet filling

15g (1 tbsp) butter
3 large cooking apples, peeled, cored and chopped into rough chunks
2 tsp Gingerbread blend (page 26)
Granulated sugar, to taste

Pancakes

2 eggs
240g (8¾oz) plain (all-purpose) flour
600ml (generous 2½ cups) milk
Large pinch of salt
2 tbsp melted butter, plus an extra 2 tsp for the pan

Makes 16 filled pancakes

Bombay Aloo with Tzatziki

Mum grew up eating Bombay Aloo in a bun, which sounds lovely, if a little carb-heavy! Instead, we're serving it with fresh tzatziki for a perfect weekday treat. You can always add a dash of cream and butter at the end if you want to fancy it up a bit.

Get your potatoes on the go, unless you have canned ones. Place the potatoes in a steamer, cover and cook for 15 minutes, or until tender. You can also boil them for 10 minutes if you don't have a steamer. You want them soft, but not falling apart. Once cooked, transfer to a bowl and set aside.

Meanwhile, make the tzatziki. Taste and adjust the seasoning to your liking. Cover and pop it in the fridge until you're ready. Before serving, you can drizzle with a drop of olive oil and sprinkle with fresh mint.

Set a heavy-bottomed frying pan (skillet) over a medium-high heat and add the vegetable oil. Once hot, gently add the tarka and allow the seeds to sizzle and pop for around 30 seconds. Watch closely and be careful not to let them burn.

Next, add the diced onion to the pan and cook for 5 minutes until it starts to colour and soften. Add the ginger-garlic paste, green chilli and salt. Stir and cook for 1 minute, then add your garam masala blend followed by the passata. Cook over a medium-high heat for another 2-3 minutes.

You will notice that the oil starts to separate. At this point, add in the steamed potatoes, cutting any that are bigger than a ping-pong ball in half. Make sure they are coated with the tomato mixture, then add the water and cook for 5-10 minutes until the sauce is reduced to a thick paste.

Turn the heat off, let everything cool and stir in your yoghurt.

If you want to make it really creamy, now is the time to add your butter or cream. Stir it through and gently warm before turning the heat off.

Sprinkle the coriander over and serve with your chilled tzatziki and perhaps some warm naan if you want something to dip into your lovely sauce.

Serves 2

400g (14oz) baby potatoes, peeled (canned potatoes also work perfectly for this dish)
½ serving of Easy Tzatziki (page 198)
2 tbsp vegetable, sunflower or rapeseed (canola) oil
1 tsp Tarka (page 28)
½ white onion, finely diced
2 tsp Ginger-Garlic Paste (page 190)
1 green chilli, minced
1 tsp salt
1 tsp Garam Masala (page 26)
3 heaped tbsp passata (strained tomatoes)
50ml (3½ tbsp) water
70g (⅓ cup) Greek-style yoghurt
25g (1½ tbsp) butter or 2 tbsp full-fat double (heavy) cream (optional)
1 tbsp roughly chopped fresh coriander (cilantro)

Za'atar Chicken with Hummus

Serves 4

4 chicken legs, skinless
Juice of ½ lemon
2 garlic cloves, minced
2 tbsp Za'atar (page 28)
2 tbsp olive oil
1 tsp sea salt

To serve
Crispy salad leaves
4 flatbreads (your favourite shop-
  bought ones for midweek)
4 tbsp Homemade Hummus
  (page 193)
Lemon wedges

This is a great midweek dish that you can prep in advance. Marinate your chicken in the morning and come home to a ready-to-bake flavour explosion. The chicken needs just 40 minutes in the oven, leaving you free to chill and enjoy your evening!

Carefully cut four slits into each of the chicken legs and place in a baking dish.

Mix together the lemon juice, garlic, za'atar, olive oil and salt. Rub this mix on the chicken, making sure to get inside the cuts.

Cover the chicken with cling film (plastic wrap) and place in the fridge for at least 30 minutes, or longer if you can.

When you are ready to get cooking, preheat the oven to 200°C fan/220°C/425°F/gas mark 7 and take the chicken out of the fridge (you don't want to put chilled chicken into the oven) and remove the cling film.

Bake for 40 minutes or until the internal temperature reaches 75°C/167°F when a meat thermometer is inserted into the thickest part of the leg. Once the chicken is cooked, allow to rest for 5 minutes before serving.

Enjoy with a crisp salad, flatbreads and a heap of your lovely homemade hummus. Finish with a squeeze of lemon.

Spice Freedom

Fiery Blackened Cajun Chicken

Ready to experiment with your spice blends? This recipe is equally amazing with: Za'atar, Jerk, Tandoori, Harissa

Olive oil, for greasing
1–2 tbsp hot chilli sauce (you know how hot you like it!)
2 heaped tbsp Cajun blend (page 25)
6–8 chicken wings
1 tbsp brown sugar
1 tbsp melted butter
1 tbsp tomato purée (paste)
½ tsp salt

Optional
1 tbsp of your favourite shop-bought mango chutney*

To serve
1 spring onion (scallion), finely sliced
Rainbow Slaw (page 196)

When I first created this recipe, it was one of those days when everything goes right. The chicken wings are crispy, fiery and succulent. But the best part is that they come out of the oven with a gorgeously sweet glaze. I love to serve them with a side of homemade rainbow slaw but you can add some crispy, roasted new potatoes to make it a more filling meal.

Preheat your oven to 200°C fan/220°C/425°F/gas mark 7.

Cover a large baking tray (sheet) with baking paper or foil (your future self will thank you when you come to wash up!) and smear with a small drizzle of olive oil.

Add your chilli sauce and Cajun blend to a large bowl. Tip in your chicken wings and stir to combine. I like to get my hands into the bowl to ensure the wings are evenly coated.

Arrange the chicken evenly on your lined tray.

Mix your sugar, melted butter and tomato purée in a separate bowl. Brush this mixture evenly over your chicken wings, then sprinkle the salt evenly on top. This will help your wings crisp up.

Put the tray in the oven and cook for 35-40 minutes until everything starts to sizzle and blacken, and your chicken is cooked thoroughly (test one piece to be sure: you want the internal temperature to reach 75°C/167°F when a meat thermometer is inserted into the thickest part of the wing).

Serve up on plates, drizzle over any remaining pan juices and sprinkle with chopped spring onion. Enjoy with a big spoonful of rainbow slaw.

*Top tip: For a really tasty twist in this dish, 5 minutes before the end of the cooking time, brush a tablespoon of mango chutney over the chicken wings and pop them back in the oven. Your chicken wings will get an additional tangy but sweet glaze and taste amazing!

Quick Rajma

Mum makes this fragrant and lightly spiced Punjabi dish about once a fortnight. Because she uses canned kidney beans, it takes no time to cook and is packed full of protein. When we go round for a big family get-together, she serves it with sweet rice... and manages to offend all the family members who have young kids, which I think is hilarious. We've included a recipe for sweet rice, but if you want, you can use plain basmati.

Set a heavy-bottomed frying pan (skillet) over a medium heat. Add the oil and, when hot, add the onion and cook until slightly browned (about 10 minutes). Stir regularly so it doesn't burn. Then add the ginger-garlic paste and fry for a further 20 seconds until the raw smell disappears.

Add your chopped tomatoes and cook down until the oil separates, stirring regularly. Once the oil has separated, add the passata and bring to a gentle simmer.

You can then stir in the salt, harissa (use more if you like your dishes hotter), Sri Lankan curry powder, garam masala and kidney beans. Add the water and simmer for 5-10 minutes. Taste, adjust the seasoning and plate up. It's that simple.

Serve with perfectly fluffy sweet rice if you want to upset the health-conscious in your family, or plain basmati if you're being 'good'.

Serves 2

2 tbsp vegetable, sunflower or rapeseed (canola) oil
1 onion, finely diced
2 tsp Ginger-Garlic Paste (page 190)
3 tomatoes, diced
4 tbsp passata (strained tomatoes)
½ tsp salt, to taste
¼ tsp Harissa (page 26)
½ tsp Sri Lankan Curry Powder (page 28)
½ tsp Garam Masala (page 26)
400g (4oz) can of kidney beans, drained but not rinsed
110ml (scant ½ cup) water
150g (5½oz) sweet rice (see 'Variation' on page 189)

Togarashi Tofu Curry Ramen

When I started writing this book, I knew it had to include a ramen dish, so I reached out to my friend Hannah at the Japan Centre food hall to collaborate. I was blown away when she said they would develop a recipe just for us. We decided to go with tofu and bring texture and flavour by crisping it up in oil with the togarashi blend. The recipe definitely calls for firm tofu to get the best results, so please do seek this out in your local supermarket.

Ramen

2–4 tbsp vegetable, sunflower or rapeseed (canola) oil, for frying
2 garlic cloves, minced
½ onion, finely diced
400g (14oz) celery, finely diced
400ml (1¾ cups) water
400ml (1¾ cups) coconut milk
3 tbsp tomato purée (paste)
60g (2¼oz) curry roux block (such as S&B Golden Curry Medium)
3 tsp Togarashi (page 28), plus extra to garnish
Pinch of salt, to taste
250g (9oz) dried ramen noodles (we recommend Itsuki ramen noodles)

Toppings

1 lime
1–2 spring onions (scallions)
1 tomato
80g (2¾oz) firm tofu
1 tsp Togarashi (page 28)

First, prepare your toppings: cut the lime into six slices and finely chop your spring onion, setting them aside for later.

Cut the tomato into four thick slices. Heat 1 tablespoon of vegetable oil in a small frying pan (skillet) and gently pan-fry the tomatoes until the edges are nicely charred. Set aside.

Dice the tofu into large cubes and mix gently with the togarashi in a bowl, being careful not to break up the pieces. Either grill (broil) the tofu or heat 2 tablespoons of oil in a heavy-bottomed frying pan and lightly fry the tofu, turning on all sides, until it is crisp at the edges. Set aside.

To make the broth, heat 1 tablespoon of oil in a large saucepan and gently cook the garlic, onion and celery until golden brown. Once browned, add the water, coconut milk and tomato purée, heat through and bring to the boil before taking off the heat. Break up the curry roux into small pieces and add to the pan with 2 teaspoons of the togarashi and the salt. Stir until the roux has melted and created a rich ramen broth.

Fill another small pan with water for the noodles and bring to the boil. Add the ramen noodles to the water and boil for 3 minutes, stirring to separate them fully - the cooking time depends on the brand and how firm you like your noodles. We recommend al dente, referred to as barikat, for extra bite. The ramen will continue to cook and soften in the broth.

Drain the noodles and share them between your bowls before pouring over the broth. Lay the togarashi tofu, charred tomato, sliced lime and chopped spring onions in groups on top of the ramen. Lastly, garnish the ramen with a final sprinkling of togarashi and enjoy. 'Itadakimasu!' as they say in Japan in recognition and appreciation of a meal.

Messy and Casual

The recipes in this chapter are for those times when you have groups of friends or family coming over and you want to serve lots of dishes on the table with bowls, plates and spoons for everyone to help themselves. Each dish is to share and everything is passed around with loads of mess and noisy chat.

There are dips and chutneys, with pitta bread or naan bread for tearing and mopping up those last bits of flavour. The key to an awesome meal like this is to offer lots of variety and textures: sauces, salad for crunch, veggie dishes for non-meat eaters and a big jug of iced punch to keep things merry.

In my home, messy and casual dinners represent the best life has to offer. So, I invite you to hang the fairy lights, get the candles burning, turn up some tunes and have fun.

Black Bean Nachos with a Fiery Salsa

These are perfect to share for a party or a night in with friends. The beans and salsa can be made a day in advance, if that's easier; all you'll need to do on the night is melt the cheese, warm the beans and serve.

Warm the oil in a saucepan. Fry the diced onion for 10 minutes until softening, then add the garlic and Mexican blend along with the beans. Stir the tomato purée and water through, then simmer for 10 minutes until the liquid has reduced.

Preheat the oven to 180°C fan/200°C/400°F/gas mark 6. Toss the grated cheeses through the corn chips and tip into a baking dish or tray. Place in the oven for about 10 minutes or until the cheese is melted and the corn chips are crisp.

Meanwhile, halve the avocado, scoop out the flesh and mash with the lime juice and salt.

To serve, spoon the beans over the corn chips and cheese, then top with the salsa. Place generous dollops of the avocado and sour cream on top.

Serve hot while the cheese is still gooey, with plenty of paper napkins.

Serves 4–6

Beans
1 tbsp vegetable, sunflower or rapeseed (canola) oil
2 small onions, diced
2 garlic cloves, crushed
1 tbsp Mexican (Tex Mex) blend (page 27)
2 x 400g (14oz) cans black beans, drained and rinsed
2 tbsp tomato purée (paste)
200ml (scant 1 cup) water

Toppings
100g (3½oz) firm mozzarella, grated
100g (3½oz) Red Leicester, Monterey Jack or Cheddar cheese, grated
200g (7oz) corn chips
1 avocado
Juice of 1 lime
Pinch of salt

To serve
100g (3½oz) Fiery Salsa (page 197)
150g (5½oz) sour cream

Banging Fish Tacos

Super-tasty and so easy to make! Allow half an hour at least for the fish to marinate – longer if possible. Pile your tacos high with colourful toppings for a delicious treat for all the family.

2 tbsp vegetable, sunflower or
   rapeseed (canola) oil
Juice and zest of 1 lime
2 garlic cloves, minced
2 tbsp Mexican (Tex-Mex) blend
   (page 27)
½ tsp salt
400g (14oz) lean white fish fillets (cod
   works brilliantly, but you can use
   whatever white fish you can
   get hold of)
8 soft tortilla wraps

Sauce
½ tsp Harissa (page 26)
Juice of 1 lime
3 tbsp mayonnaise
150g (5½oz) sour cream
1 garlic clove, minced
Generous pinch of salt

Additional toppings
Pickled Red Onions (page 195)
100g (3½oz) white cabbage, finely
   shredded (or use crunchy iceberg
   lettuce if that's what you prefer)
1 red or green chilli, deseeded and
   finely chopped
A good handful of freshly chopped
   coriander (cilantro)
1 avocado, chopped
Lime wedges

Use a large, non-metallic bowl to mix together the oil, lime juice and zest, garlic, Mexican blend and salt. Add your fish, stir gently to combine and leave to marinate for around 1 hour. Longer is better, if you can.

Meanwhile, make your sauce by mixing all the ingredients together in a bowl. Keep in the fridge until ready to serve.

Next, prepare all your topping ingredients. Squeeze a little lime juice over the avocado to stop it from spoiling. You can arrange your toppings on one platter, or serve at the table in individual bowls - whatever works for you! Keep in the fridge until needed.

When you are ready to get cooking, preheat your oven to 200°C fan/220°C/425°F/gas mark 7 and lightly grease a baking tray (sheet). Put the fish and all of the marinade on the tray and cook for around 15 minutes (the cooking time depends on the thickness of the fish, so make sure you check it is cooked through).

Remove the tray from the oven and gently flake the fish apart using two forks. If it doesn't flake easily, return it to the oven for a few more minutes.

Warm the tortilla wraps according to the packet instructions.

Spoon the fish onto the warmed tortillas, with your lovely sauce drizzled over, and pile high with your choice of toppings.

Legendary Tandoori Chicken

Serves 4

An all-time Indian classic and definitely one of our family favourites: we bring you the legendary tandoori chicken! Please note the time needed for marinating the chicken; it's definitely worth it for the flavour.

700g (1lb 9oz) chicken thighs, skin off, bone-in (or 500g/1lb 2oz boneless)
2 tbsp Ginger-Garlic Paste (page 190)
1 tsp salt
4 tbsp Greek-style yoghurt
2 tsp Tandoori Masala (page 27)
1 tbsp vegetable, sunflower or rapeseed (canola) oil
2 tbsp lime juice

To serve
4 pitta breads or wraps, warmed
Crispy salad leaves
4 tsp Zingy Mint and Coriander Chutney (page 198)
4 tbsp Garlic Yoghurt (page 193)

Mix the chicken with the ginger-garlic paste and salt, cover, and leave in the fridge for at least 30 minutes so the flavours can develop. Meanwhile, combine the yoghurt with the tandoori masala, oil and lime juice in a large non-metallic bowl.

After 30 minutes, add the chicken to the spiced yoghurt, cover once again and pop back in the fridge to marinate for 2-3 hours (or longer if you can).

When it's time to cook, preheat your grill (broiler) to medium-high. Add the chicken thighs and grill for 8-10 minutes, turning regularly, taking care not to burn them.

Slice the largest piece in the middle to see if the juices run clear; if they don't, continue to grill for a couple of minutes longer.

Serve immediately onto warm pittas or wraps, then pile on some crispy salad leaves, zingy chutney and the garlic yoghurt.

Street-style Pav Bhaji with a Soft Bread Roll

This is such an incredible street-food dish and the perfect way to bring the taste of Mumbai to your kitchen. It's humble, but, because it's served on a buttery toasted bun, it's really decadent and filling. Mum and Dad literally arranged family holidays for us to Mumbai to go to the street seller and then eat Pav Bhaji on the beach, so this dish really does remind me of great family times.

Chop the potato, carrots, cauliflower and sweet potato into similarly sized chunks. Steam or boil until they are soft, then mash to form a smooth consistency. You might want to start the potatoes off first as they will take a little longer than the rest.

Heat the oil in a large heavy-bottomed frying pan (skillet) over a medium heat. Fry the onion for about 5 minutes, then add the ginger-garlic paste. Cook for a minute, stirring regularly, then add the diced tomatoes, salt and Sri Lankan curry powder. Stir thoroughly and continue to cook over a medium heat for about 5 minutes to allow the flavours to combine.

Add your veggie mash and petits pois and stir. Continue to fry for 10 minutes until your mixture looks like a dry paste.

Meanwhile, slice the bread rolls in half. Heat another frying pan over a medium heat and add 1 teaspoon of the butter. Once it's melted, fry the rolls in the butter for a minute or so on each side, until lightly toasted but not burned.

Add the remaining butter to the vegetable mash, stir and then serve the mash piled onto warm buttery buns with a squeeze of lime juice, a sprinkling of fresh coriander and your choice of toppings. Bliss.

Serves 4

1 potato, peeled
2 carrots, peeled
4 cauliflower florets
½ sweet potato, peeled
2 tbsp vegetable, sunflower or rapeseed (canola) oil
1 white onion, diced
2 tsp Ginger-Garlic Paste (page 190)
3 tomatoes, diced
1 tsp salt
2 tsp Sri Lankan Curry Powder (page 28)
50g (1¾oz) frozen petits pois

To serve
2 soft white bread rolls
45g (3 tbsp) butter
Lime, for squeezing
1 tbsp freshly chopped coriander (cilantro)

Optional toppings
Crispy fried onions
Tamarind Chutney (page 197)
Zingy Mint and Coriander Chutney (page 198)
1 red onion, finely diced
Bombay mix or sev
Freshly chopped green chillies (1 or 2 according to how hot you like it)

Barbecued Corn with Harissa and Lime

Serves 4 as a side

4 corn on the cob with husks
4 tbsp Greek-style yoghurt
2 tsp Harissa (page 26)
1 tsp Baharat (page 25)
Zest and juice of 1 lime, plus extra
  to serve
1 tbsp freshly chopped coriander
  (cilantro)

Your tastebuds are going to love the contrasting flavours of sweet barbecued (grilled) corn combined with fiery chilli and tangy lime.

Soak the corn - husks and all - in cold water for 30 minutes before cooking.

Mix the Greek-style yoghurt with the harissa, baharat, salt and lime zest and juice.

When you are ready to get cooking, fire up the barbecue (grill). If you don't have one or it's raining, the cobs, still in their husks, can be cooked in the oven (preheated to 220°C fan/240°C/475°F/gas mark 9) for 15 minutes or on a smoking-hot griddle (grill) pan, turning every so often for about 15 minutes.

Once cooked, peel back the husk and brush the cobs with the yoghurt mix.

Sprinkle the chopped coriander on top and squeeze over more lime juice before serving.

Tex-Mex Beef Burger with Guacamole

Mexico meets America. If you're hankering after some big Tex-Mex flavours, this homemade burger will not let you down. Pile it high with toppings and a few crushed tortilla chips for some texture and crunch. Allow an hour for the Tex-Mex blend to flavour the meat and the cabbage to pickle.

Patties
500g (1lb 2oz) minced (ground) beef (ideally around 20% fat)
1 tbsp Mexican (Tex-Mex) blend (page 27)
1 tbsp vegetable, sunflower or rapeseed (canola) oil

Pickle
½ white cabbage, thick stalk removed
100ml (scant ½ cup) white wine vinegar
2 tsp flaky salt

To serve
4 burger buns, split
100ml (scant ½ cup) sour cream
4 tbsp Easy Guacamole (page 193)
50g (1¾oz) tortilla chips
Handful of fresh coriander (cilantro)

Spread out the minced beef and sprinkle with the spice blend. Mix it through but try not to over-handle the meat - your warm hands will start to melt the fat. Put the meat back in the fridge for at least an hour.

Shred the cabbage finely and put in a bowl. In a small saucepan, bring the vinegar and salt to a simmer with 100ml (scant ½ cup) water, then pour over the cabbage. Leave to sit for an hour.

Once the meat and spice blend have had their time, divide into four evenly shaped patties. Heat the oil in a frying pan (skillet) until hot, then place the patties in it. Cook for 5 minutes on one side, flip over and brown on the other side and cook until the inside is done to your liking.

Finally, assemble. Spread the base of a burger bun with a smear of sour cream, top with some of the cabbage (squeeze it first, so it isn't too wet), then place a patty on top. Finish with the guacamole, then roughly crush some tortilla chips and sprinkle them on top along with some coriander. Serve topped with the other half of the burger bun and any remaining cabbage pickle or guacamole on the side. Also, go large with some fries if you're in need of a big meal.

Lamb Shawarma

Me and my friend Pete have a tradition of getting everything prepared for this dish, putting it in the oven and then drinking beer until it's cooked. Life has changed so much since we were young, and now that we have serious jobs and families, we don't get to see one another very often. This is our tradition, and making this dish together is always a good opportunity for a proper catch-up. Because the lamb is cooked long and slow to become properly tender, we can end up pretty merry by the time we get to eat it. This dish benefits from being marinated the day or even two days before you plan to eat.

Blend together the oil, onion, garlic, lemon juice, baharat and salt with a stick blender.

Rub this over the lamb and marinate in the fridge in a sealed bag for 24 hours, or 48 hours if you can.

When it's time to get cooking, preheat your oven to 140°C fan/180°C/350°F/gas mark 4.

Pour the hot chicken stock into a roasting dish and add your lamb and all of the marinade. Cover with foil and cook for 4 hours, basting every 30 minutes. If the stock dries out, top up with a little water.

Let the lamb rest, covered with foil, for 10 minutes.

Serve on a platter in the centre of the table, sprinkled with the fresh mint. I like to carve at the table and then let everyone dive in and build their own kebabs with the pitta, salad, pickled onions and yoghurt.

100ml (scant ½ cup) olive oil
1 onion, peeled and roughly chopped
2 garlic cloves
Juice of 1 lemon
3 tsp Baharat (page 25)
1 tsp salt
½ leg of lamb (roughly 1kg/2lb 4oz)
500ml (2 cups) hot chicken stock (bouillon)

To serve
Bunch of fresh mint, leaves picked and roughly chopped
4 pitta breads
Salad – whatever you fancy; I love crisp Iceberg, cucumber and sliced tomatoes with a squeeze of fresh lemon
Pickled Red Onions (page 195)
2 tbsp Garlic Yoghurt (page 193)

A Reuben-esque!

The only real work involved is in making your slaw – the rest is just assembly! The slaw dressing is based on the Russian dressing that is usually spread thickly on a classic Reuben, but this has its roots in a big sharing-style sub too.

Slaw

2 carrots, peeled, trimmed and
  julienned
¼ head white cabbage, core removed,
  finely shredded
2 tbsp cider vinegar
Pinch of salt

Dressing

1 tbsp ketchup
3 tbsp mayonnaise
2 tsp pickle juice from the jar of
  pickled cucumbers
½ tsp Worcestershire sauce
1 tsp Harissa (page 26)

The rest

1 baguette (fresh or baked at home)
100–300g (3½–10½oz) sliced
  pastrami (this is very much down
  to taste)
125g (4½oz) grated Monterey Jack
  or other hard cheese such as
  Red Leicester
A small jar of sliced pickled cucumbers

Put the prepared carrots and cabbage in a bowl with the vinegar and salt and give them a good squeeze with your hands, until the cabbage feels a little softer. Set aside for 10 minutes while you work on the rest of the sandwich.

If you are baking the baguette, pop it in the oven following the instructions on the packet. Once it's done, switch your oven to grill (broil), or turn on the grill (broiler) if the baguette didn't need baking.

Whisk together all the dressing ingredients in a big bowl, taste and adjust the seasoning if you want more heat (harissa) or sweetness (pickle juice) and set aside.

Once the cabbage and carrot have had their time, squeeze them very well over the sink. The salt will have drawn water out and you don't want your sandwich to be soggy, so keep squeezing until the shreds are noticeably drier. Stir them through the dressing.

Finally, assemble the sandwich. Slice the baguette along one side and pull it open. Layer in the pastrami and then sprinkle the cheese over the top. Transfer to the grill until the cheese has melted. Top with as many pickles as you fancy, then add a generous layer of the slaw. Bring the whole baguette to the table and slice into portions.

Harissa, Garlic and Coriander Swirl Bread

Serves 4 as a side or accompaniment to a meal

Flour, for dusting

300g (10½oz) risen white bread dough, after its first prove (a third of the recipe on page 185)

1 x quantity Flavour-bomb Harissa Paste (page 199)

15g (1oz) fresh coriander (cilantro)

1 large garlic clove

2 tbsp olive oil

Pinch of salt

If this bread doesn't impress your guests, then literally nothing will. Sack them all and get better friends!

Line a 23-cm (9-in) round cake tin (cake pan) with baking paper or a liner.

Flour your work surface and knock back the dough; leave to rest for 10 minutes.

Shape it roughly into a rectangle and then roll it into a rectangle about 60 x 30cm (24 x 12in).

Spread the harissa paste thinly and evenly over the dough and then roll from the long end into a long sausage. Use a sharp knife to cut the dough into 16 pieces.

Starting in the middle of your cake tin, place the first piece so you can see the swirl, and place five pieces in a circle around this first piece, leaving small gaps between to allow for proving (the pieces will join up, but this allows the bread to rise properly). Place the remaining pieces in a circle around this in the same way.

Cover gently with a clean dish towel and leave to rise for 30 minutes.

Preheat the oven to 220°C fan/240°C/475°F/gas mark 9.

Bake in the centre of the oven for 35-40 minutes. Keep an eye on it and, if it is beginning to colour too much, slightly dampen a piece of baking paper, scrunch it up, unwrap and place gently over the bread.

Meanwhile, chop the coriander, crush the garlic and mix into the oil, seasoning with a little salt.

Remove the bread and, if serving immediately, use a pastry brush to baste it with the garlic-infused oil. Alternatively, if the bread is for a later time, allow it to cool, then wrap in foil and pop it into a warm oven for 10 minutes, basting with the oil before serving.

Everyone's Happy Pizza

Pizza is a great choice for a party. You can customize toppings to suit everyone; and the Easy Pizza Dough and the Big Batch Tomato Sauce recipes are simple enough to complement anything you fancy adding. We've included some of our favourite combinations as suggestions below, but feel free to be as creative as you like!

Prepare the dough following the method on page 186.

When you are ready to get cooking, tip the dough onto a floured work surface and knock some of the air out of it. Divide the dough into six and shape each into a ball. Roll out to 5mm (¼in) thick on sheets of baking paper so you can easily slide the pizza bases onto a baking sheet.

Turn your oven to its highest temperature. Spread one of the bases with a couple of tablespoons of tomato sauce, then a layer of grated cheese and whatever toppings you fancy. Don't overload it, or the base will struggle to cook properly. Repeat until you've topped all your bases.

Bake each pizza one at a time on the top shelf of the oven for about 12 minutes, until the crust is a deep golden brown. Keep an eye on them; if your oven is particularly hot, they may be cooked even faster.

Flour, for dusting
1 x quantity Easy Pizza Dough (page 186)
250ml (generous 1 cup) Big Batch Tomato Sauce (page 187)
400g (14oz) firm mozzarella, grated

Topping suggestions
Go for whatever you fancy, but here are a few of my go-to combos:
– Anchovies, mozzarella, chilli flakes (red pepper flakes) with basil and a drizzle of olive oil added after baking
– Spicy chicken, red onion, chargrilled red (bell) pepper
– Ham, pineapple, chopped fresh parsley
– Asparagus, goat's cheese, thinly sliced fennel

Makes 6 pizzas

Aloo Tikki with a Rainbow Slaw

Aloo tikki is a really popular Indian street-food dish. They're so easy to make, and Mum made these tikkis when I was growing up precisely for this reason. I love their versatility, as you can have them with chutney as a starter or pile them into buns burger-fashion and serve with salad for a main.

Here I am serving the tikkis with a lovely chickpea curry and a zingy rainbow slaw for freshness.

Tikkis
6 floury potatoes, peeled, steamed and mashed*
3 tbsp freshly chopped coriander (cilantro), plus extra to garnish
2 tsp salt
½ red onion, finely diced
1 tsp Garam Masala (page 26)
1 tsp Harissa, but if you want more heat, then go for it! (page 26)
2 tbsp vegetable, sunflower or rapeseed (canola) oil, for frying

Sauce
8 heaped tbsp Mamma Spice's Famous Chickpea Curry (page 64)

To serve
Rainbow Slaw (page 196)
Tamarind Chutney (optional) (page 197)

Put the mashed potatoes, fresh coriander, half the salt, the red onion, garam masala and harissa into a large bowl. Stir thoroughly to combine your ingredients. Taste and add more salt or harissa at this stage if you feel the mixture needs it.

Make the tikkis by splitting the mashed potato mixture into 6 or 8 individual portions. Shape them into flat mini burgers, not too thick, otherwise they won't cook through to the middle without burning.

Heat a heavy-bottomed frying pan (skillet) over a medium heat. Add the vegetable oil and fry your tikkis until they are browned. This should take about 2-3 minutes on each side but keep an eye on them as you want them to brown but not burn.

Meanwhile, gently heat the chickpea curry in a small pan over a medium heat. Add a little water if the mixture is too thick.

Serve the tikkis on a plate with the sauce and the rainbow slaw on the side. You can finish off with a sprinkling of freshly chopped coriander and some lovely tamarind chutney if you have some.

*Top tip: Because you've steamed rather than boiled the potatoes, they shouldn't be watery, but if they are, you can add a tablespoon of breadcrumbs to soak up the moisture.

Spicy Lamb and Baharat Parcels

Serves 2

250g (9oz) minced (ground) lamb
1 egg, beaten
½ tsp salt
1 onion, finely chopped
2 garlic cloves, minced
1 tsp Baharat (page 25)
Flour, for dusting
1 x 320g (11¼oz) ready-rolled puff
   pastry sheet or 6 sheets of filo
   (phyllo) pastry
2 tbsp Flavour-bomb Harissa Paste
   (page 199)
1 tsp Za'atar, for sprinkling (page 28)

To serve
Handful of coriander (cilantro),
   finely chopped, optional
2 tbsp Janey's Crunchy Carrot Relish
   (page 194)

Puff pastry is so lovely and buttery and it works well with this harissa-spiced lamb filling. You might, however, want to reduce the amount of harissa paste if you're not a fan of fiery food.

Preheat the oven to 180°C fan/200°C/400°F/gas mark 4.

In a bowl, add the lamb, beaten egg (reserve a little to glaze the parcels at the end), salt, onion, garlic and baharat and mix until combined.

Divide the mixture into six and form them into balls.

Lightly flour your work surface, unroll the sheet of pastry and cut into six squares. Put about ½ teaspoon of the harissa paste into the centre of each square and spread out with the back of the spoon in a circle, roughly the same size as the balls of filling.

Put a ball of the mixture in the middle of each square then fold each corner of the pastry to meet in the centre, squeezing together in the centre.

Baste the top with the reserved beaten egg, then sprinkle each parcel with a little za'atar.

Bake for 20-25 minutes and serve immediately, scattered with fresh coriander, if liked, and a spoonful each of the lovely carrot relish.

Hilina's Doro Wot (Ethiopian Chicken and Egg Stew)

Doro Wot is a traditional Ethiopian stew using berbere that we've eaten in my family for many years. It's a warming, comforting one-pot dish which is humble, full of flavour and great for sharing. This recipe, however, has been kindly shared by my good friend Hilina Burke, who runs the incredible Abyssinia Kitchen based on the Wirral in Merseyside. Hilina is an absolute master of Ethiopian food and so it's a real honour to include one of her dishes in this book.

Mix the chicken with 1 tablespoon of the berbere in a large bowl. Stir to combine thoroughly.

Heat 2 tablespoons of the oil and the butter in a large, heavy-bottomed frying pan (skillet) over a medium heat. Fry the chicken pieces on all sides until brown. Set aside.

Heat the remaining oil in a separate frying pan. Gently fry your onions until lightly browned, then add your tomato purée and the rest of the berbere.

Reduce the heat to the lowest it will go and cook for 20 minutes, stirring regularly, so the onions don't burn. You can add some butter to the pan if it gets a little dry.

Next, add your ginger-garlic paste and the chicken, stir and cook for a further 25 minutes. Again, stir regularly over a very low heat and add more butter if the mixture is catching.

Meanwhile, boil your eggs in a separate saucepan for 8 minutes. Once cooked, run under cold water and leave in the pan covered with fresh cold water.

After the 25 minutes is up, add the water and salt to your pan with the chicken and cook for a further 10 minutes.

Shell the boiled eggs and add them to the sauce. Cook until warmed through (around 5 minutes). Taste for seasoning and add more salt if you think your sauce needs it.

Garnish with the fresh coriander and serve with the steaming hot rice.

Serves 3

6 skinless chicken thighs
2 tbsp Berbere (page 25)
4 tbsp vegetable, sunflower or rapeseed (canola) oil
15g (1 tbsp) butter, plus extra as needed
4 large onions, very finely diced
200g (7oz) tomato purée (paste)
1 tbsp Ginger-Garlic Paste (page 190)
4 eggs
500ml (2 cups) water
½ tsp salt, to taste
2 tbsp fresh coriander, roughly chopped, to serve
150g (5½oz) Perfectly Fluffy Rice (page 189), to serve

'Fakeaway' Salt and Pepper Chicken and Chips

Our little family business, Spice Kitchen, is based in Liverpool and in these parts 'salt and pepper' anything is a BIG deal. So there was no way we were going to get away with leaving this recipe out! The time needed for marinating the chicken is well worth it, so please don't skip this step!

4 skinless chicken breasts, cut into bite-sized chunks
2 egg whites
75g (2½oz) plain (all-purpose) flour
75g (2½oz) cornflour (cornstarch)
1 tsp baking powder

Sauce
4 tbsp vegetable, sunflower or rapeseed (canola) oil
2 tsp Ginger-Garlic Paste (page 190)
2 red chillies, minced
1 onion, diced
1 red (bell) pepper, diced
1 green (bell) pepper, diced
2 tbsp dark soy sauce

Spice mix
1 tsp Chinese Seven Spice (page 25)
½ tsp Harissa (page 26)
Pinch of white pepper, to taste
1 tsp sugar

Chips
500g (1lb 2oz) floury potatoes, unpeeled, washed and dried on paper towels
1 tbsp salt
1 tbsp sunflower or vegetable oil

To serve (optional)
2 spring onions (scallions), chopped
1 tbsp sesame seeds

This is a recipe of halves! So when you prep the ingredients for the sauce it's good to mix the diced onion and peppers in a bowl then separate them into two bowls. The same goes for the ginger-garlic paste and minced chillies.

Mix all the ingredients for the spice mix in a small bowl. Stir to combine, then separate into two bowls.

Next, marinate your chicken. Take a large bowl and mix together the egg whites and half the spice mix. Stir to combine with the chicken, cover and leave in your fridge for 30 minutes to an hour.

Towards the end of the marinating time, preheat the oven to 190°C fan/210°C/410°F/gas mark 6½ and line a decent-sized baking tray (sheet) with baking paper.

Meanwhile, cut your potatoes into thick chips (fries) and parboil them in a large pan of boiling water with a pinch of the salt for 5-10 minutes, or until slightly tender. Drain and set aside, leaving them to steam themselves dry.

Mix the plain flour, cornflour and baking powder in a large bowl, then add the chicken with all of the marinade, ensuring that each piece is coated. Spread evenly onto the lined baking tray.

Lightly grease a separate baking tray with a little oil. Arrange your chips in a single, even layer and drizzle over the tablespoon of oil and evenly scrunch over the remaining salt. Bake the chips and chicken for 20-25 minutes until crispy. Depending on how thick you've cut your chips, they might need longer; you know how you like them.

When the chicken is done (check that the juices run clear), remove from the oven and set aside.

For the sauce, heat a wok over a high heat. Add 2 tablespoons of the oil and wait for it to get really hot. When you're ready, add half the ginger-garlic paste and chilli and allow to sizzle for about 10 seconds, stirring regularly, so they don't burn. Add half the diced onion and peppers and the remaining spice mix. Continue to fry for about 2 minutes before adding half the soy sauce. Lastly, add the cooked chips, stir and continue to fry for 2 minutes until everything is combined. You've just made salt and pepper chips!

You can pop your chips back on their baking tray and keep them warm in the oven (which will still be hot) while you cook the chicken.

Get the wok back on the heat and add the remaining 2 tablespoons of oil. Once hot, add the remaining ginger-garlic paste and chilli. Sizzle for 20 seconds, then add the onions and peppers, cooking as before. Add the remaining soy sauce, then the cooked chicken and fry for 3 minutes until everything is combined.

Then, plate up! I like to scatter over chopped spring onions for a nod of greenery. You can also throw over some sesame seeds for garnish.

Baked Feta with a Spiced Flatbread

Spice Freedom

If you've got friends or family coming round for cocktails, then this dish is great to serve when everyone arrives. And, while we understand you are mega-busy, if you can carve out a little time to make these flatbreads from scratch, we promise you won't regret it. They are simple to make but you do need 1½ hours for proving the dough.

If you're making your own, get started on the flatbreads. Tip the flour into a large mixing bowl and add the salt and spices on one side and the yeast on the other. Combine the yoghurt and the water, pour into the bowl and mix into the flour to form a dough. Cover the bowl with a damp dish towel and leave to swell in size for 45 minutes.

Meanwhile, slice the carrots into ribbons with a swivel-head peeler. Put them into a bowl. Bring the vinegar to a simmer with the salt, sugar and za'atar, and pour over the carrots. Set aside to pickle.

Once the dough is plump and risen, wet your hand and then knead the bread inside the bowl. Fold it over itself, turning the bowl as you do so, wetting your hand again if it begins to stick. Once you've knocked the air out of the dough, and it is soft and smooth, cover the bowl again and leave for 45 minutes.

While the dough is proving, prepare the feta. Place the blocks on a sheet of foil and drizzle with the oil. Sprinkle the spice mix generously over the top and add the lemon zest and salt. Seal with the foil to make feta parcels and place on a tray, ready for baking.

Preheat your oven to 220°C fan/240°C/475°F/gas mark 9 and line a baking tray (sheet) with baking paper.

Tip the risen dough out of the bowl and cut into eight even pieces. Flour your work surface and roll each piece out into as round a shape as possible, about 5mm (¼in) thick. Transfer each to the lined tray, then place the bread and the feta trays in the oven. Bake the breads for 7-9 minutes, until golden and puffed. Wrap in a dish towel to keep warm while you give the feta another 15 minutes. Bring the feta straight from the oven to the table, sprinkle over a little coriander and serve with the warm breads and your pickles.

Ready to experiment with your blends? This recipe is equally amazing with: Harissa, Berbere, Baharat, Ras el Hanout

400g (14oz) feta
2 tbsp vegetable, sunflower or rapeseed (canola) oil
1 tbsp Za'atar (page 28)
Zest of 1 unwaxed lemon
Generous pinch of salt
Coriander (cilantro) leaves, to garnish

Flatbread
400g (14oz) strong white bread flour
10g (¼oz) salt
2 tsp Za'atar (page 28)
1 x 7g sachet (1 tsp) fast-action yeast
120g (4¼oz) yoghurt
150ml (scant ⅔ cup) lukewarm water

Quick pickle carrots
3 carrots, peeled
100ml (scant ½ cup) cider vinegar
1 tbsp table salt
1 tsp granulated sugar
2 tsp Za'atar (page 28)

Makes enough for 6-8

Kebab Day

400g (14oz) boneless, skinless chicken thighs, cut into bite-sized pieces
2 tbsp olive oil, plus extra for greasing
1 red onion, cut into wedges
1 courgette (zucchini), sliced thickly into rounds
1 red (bell) pepper, deseeded and cut into chunks
10 cherry tomatoes

Marinade
1 tbsp Baharat (page 25)
½ tsp Harissa (page 26)
4 tbsp Greek-style yoghurt
½ tsp salt
3 garlic cloves, minced
Juice of 1 lemon
Freshly ground black pepper, to taste

To serve
Pittas
Garlic Yoghurt (page 193)
Pickled Red Onions (page 195)
Iceberg lettuce, shredded
½ lemon, cut into wedges
Your favourite hot chilli sauce (optional)

You will need
Bamboo or metal skewers (if using bamboo skewers, soak them in cold water for at least 30 minutes before using)

Ann, the person who helped me to write this book, told me that the day her now wife proposed to her, instead of going out for a fancy meal, they sat and ate a homemade kebab and planned their elopement wedding. Ann and Lyn call that day 'Kebab Day' and it got me thinking that everyone needs an amazing recipe in their lives for those moments when nothing except a good old kebab will do.

My recipe uses chicken, but if you're vegetarian or following a plant-based diet then you can swap this out for portobello mushrooms, tofu or even seitan. Whatever you use, marinate it for at least 2 hours in this spicy mix for a culinary marriage made in heaven.

Put the marinade ingredients into a large, non-metallic bowl and stir thoroughly to combine. Add the chicken and turn to coat the pieces. Cover with cling film (plastic wrap) and leave in the fridge for at least 2 hours, but overnight if you can.

When you are ready to get cooking, preheat your grill (broiler) to medium-high. Cover a baking tray (sheet) with foil and oil lightly.

Coat your skewers with the oil and then thread the marinated chicken, alternating it with the vegetables.

Place the kebabs on your baking tray and then grill (broil), turning every couple of minutes until the chicken is thoroughly cooked, about 6-8 minutes depending on the thickness of your pieces. You can baste the chicken with more marinade each time you turn. Check one piece to make sure it is cooked and no longer pink inside before removing from the heat.

A couple of minutes before the end of cooking, gently warm your pittas under the grill on both sides, taking care not to let them burn.

Serve the chicken and vegetables in the pittas with lashings of garlic yoghurt, red onions and some lettuce for crunch. Finish with a squeeze of lemon and some hot sauce if you wish.

Spiced Tequila Pineapple

Serves 4–6

1 large pineapple, or 1 x 435g (15oz) can of pineapples slices, drained
60g (4 tbsp) butter
4 tbsp dark brown sugar
1–2 tsp Harissa (page 26)
4 tbsp tequila
Pinch of salt

This is a great dessert for a party. It's fantastic with fresh pineapple, but it's good with canned too, if that's what you can get your hands on. Serve with vanilla ice cream, crème fraîche, or softly whipped cream.

To prepare a fresh pineapple, twist the crown close to the base and pull it off. Trim the top and base, so your pineapple is stable and flat on both ends. Trim off the skin, removing the spikes from the flesh. Slice into 2-cm (¾-in) thick rounds.

In a wide flat frying pan (skillet), melt the butter until starting to foam. Whisk in the sugar and cook for a couple of minutes. Add the harissa, tequila and pinch of salt and cook until bubbling gently.

Add the pineapple to the pan and cook until caramelized on both sides - about 5 minutes a side.

Serve a slice topped with some of the sauce from the pan and either cream or ice cream.

Fancy Dinners

We are all busy, and most of us are looking for time-saving tips for most of our meals. But there are occasions, whether they be a date night or family or friends coming over, that we are prepared to go the extra mile. The recipes in this section are for those times.

Chilli Paneer Sakonis-style

I owe my love of this incredible dish to Sakonis restaurant in London. When I was 7 or 8, I travelled alone on the National Express coach from Birmingham to visit my aunt and uncle (I still can't believe my parents let me do that!) and would always ask to go to Sakonis for their awesome chilli paneer.

When I got back home to Birmingham, I would pester my mum to make this dish 'Sakonis-style' and, to her credit, she smashed it every time. To this day, it remains a signature dish at Sakonis and this is our take on it. I hope you love it.

Put the paneer, tandoori masala, yoghurt, salt, garlic if using, chilli and harissa into a bowl. Stir to combine and then leave to marinate for about 10 minutes.

Heat the oil and butter in a heavy-bottomed frying pan (skillet) over a medium heat. Once sizzling, add the paneer and all of the marinade. The yoghurt will split, but don't worry.

Fry the paneer on one side and then turn once, being careful not to burn. It will probably need 2-3 minutes on each side. Check for seasoning and add more salt and tandoori masala if you want more flavour.

Once cooked, take the paneer cubes out of the pan and set aside in a bowl.

Keep the pan over a medium heat and add a splash of water to loosen the crusty bits from the bottom. Add the chopped red peppers and fry in the lovely buttery spices. The water will evaporate as you cook and stir. Fry for about 3-4 minutes so that the peppers are cooked, but not so much that they entirely lose their crunch.

Transfer the peppers into a bowl, pile on your paneer and finish with chopped coriander.

200g (7oz) paneer, cut into cubes
3 tsp Tandoori Masala (page 27), plus extra as needed
3 tbsp Greek-style yoghurt
½ tsp salt
2 garlic cloves, minced (optional)
½ green chilli, minced
½ tsp Harissa (page 26)
2 tsp vegetable, sunflower or rapeseed (canola) oil
10g (scant 1 tbsp) butter
2 red (bell) peppers, deseeded and cut into chunks
1 tsp chopped fresh coriander (cilantro)

Serves 4 as a starter

Baked Trout with Baharat, Tomato and Lemon

This easy baked trout recipe always goes down a storm in our house! Keeping the fish whole means that it retains its moisture and that it cooks to perfection. Prep the trout in advance as it needs to sit in the fridge for a couple of hours.

2 whole trout, gutted, scaled and cleaned (you can ask your fishmonger to do this)
1 tsp salt
2 tbsp Baharat (page 25)
2 tbsp olive oil
2 tomatoes, sliced
1 lemon, sliced

Salad
1 red onion, finely sliced
3 tbsp black olives, sliced
5cm (2in) cucumber, sliced into rounds
2 tomatoes, sliced
1 tbsp cider vinegar
1 tbsp olive oil
Salt, to taste

Clean the fish well, wash and pat dry with paper towel. Score on both sides and rub with the salt.

Mix the baharat with the olive oil and smear all over and inside the trout.

Place the slices of tomato and lemon inside and over the trout. Wrap the fish loosely in foil, creating an envelope and sealing the open edges. Put in the fridge for a couple of hours.

Preheat your oven to 220°C fan/240°C/475°F/gas mark 9. Place the foil envelope on a baking tray (sheet) and put into the oven for 15 minutes, then carefully open the foil and cook for another 5 minutes.

While your trout is baking, make the salad by mixing all the ingredients together in a bowl, and season to your liking.

Serve the trout in its parcel, with all of its baking juices, and the salad, together with a chilled glass of white.

Saag Gosht

Growing up, I have amazing memories of going to restaurants in Birmingham where we all shared this dish and ate straight from the pan, scooping up the sauce with naan bread. So, I couldn't write this book without shouting about saag (spinach) dishes. This recipe is an adaptation of many I've tried over the years. For maximum flavour, marinating the lamb overnight is preferable, but even if you can leave it for 2–3 hours it will be worth it.

Put the diced lamb into a bowl and mix in the ginger-garlic paste. Cover and marinate in the fridge overnight or for a couple of hours at least.

When it's time to cook, place a heavy-bottomed frying pan (skillet) over a medium heat and add 3 tablespoons of the oil. Once hot, add the tarka and allow the seeds to sizzle and pop for about 30 seconds, being careful not to burn them. Add the onions to the pan, stir, and add a good pinch of salt and the sugar (if using) to help them cook down and caramelize. Fry over a low-medium heat for about 20 minutes until the onions have taken on a golden-brown colour, stirring regularly. Once cooked, take the pan off the heat and transfer the onions to a bowl using a slotted spoon. Allow to cool for 5-10 minutes.

Next, put the cooked onions, diced tomatoes, ginger-garlic paste, chillies, garam masala and tandoori masala into a blender and blitz to a lovely smooth paste.

Add the remaining oil to the frying pan over a medium heat. Add the tomato and onion paste and fry for about 8 minutes. It may spit, so keep stirring and adjust the heat down if needed.

Add the harissa and the lamb. Fry over a medium-high heat for a further 5-10 minutes until the lamb is sealed on all sides and coated with the paste. Add the water and bring to a gentle simmer. Cover and cook for about an hour, stirring regularly.

Next, add your frozen spinach to the pan and continue to cook for another hour, again stirring regularly, until the lamb is tender. You can check for seasoning and add more salt and chilli at this stage, if you think your sauce needs it. Serve with naan bread and loads of freshly chopped coriander.

Serves 4

500g (1lb 2oz) boneless diced lamb
1 tbsp Ginger-Garlic Paste (page 190)

Sauce
6 tbsp vegetable, sunflower or rapeseed (canola) oil
1 tsp Tarka (page 28)
3 onions, peeled and very thinly sliced into half-moons
1 tsp salt, to taste
1 tsp sugar (optional)
200g (7oz) fresh tomatoes, diced
1 tbsp Ginger-Garlic Paste (page 190)
1–2 green chillies, roughly chopped, to taste
1 tsp Garam Masala (page 26)
1 tsp Tandoori Masala (page 27)
½ tsp Harissa (page 26)
150ml (scant ⅔ cup) cold water
400g (14oz) frozen spinach

To serve
Easy Midweek Naan (page 186)
Small bunch of coriander (cilantro), roughly chopped

Mamma Spice's Dal Makhani

Serves 4

Mum always has a batch of dal in her freezer to pull out for a quick midweek meal. But back home in India, this recipe was made by her mum only on special occasions due to the extra time needed for soaking the lentils and gathering together the ingredients. Pick a day when you can really indulge yourself in the experience of cooking this recipe from scratch. You won't regret it.

250g (9oz) whole black urad dal

2 tbsp vegetable, sunflower or rapeseed (canola) oil

1 onion, finely diced

2 tsp Ginger-Garlic Paste (page 190)

½ green chilli, minced

2 tsp Garam Masala (page 26)

1 tsp Sri Lankan Curry Powder (page 28)

2 fresh tomatoes, chopped

4 tbsp passata (strained tomatoes)

Salt, to taste

2 tsp chopped fresh coriander (cilantro)

10g (scant 1 tbsp) butter (optional)

1 tbsp double (heavy) cream

Rinse the dal thoroughly. Tip into a large saucepan and fill with water. Turn on the heat, bring to a rolling simmer and cook for 3 hours. Keep a close eye on this, topping up the water now and then, so the pan doesn't boil dry. Alternatively, if you have a pressure cooker, the dal will only take 20-30 minutes to soften. You'll notice the water becomes dark and starts to take on the consistency of thin soup.

Set aside the dal, together with its cooking water (it's packed with flavour, so please don't pour it away!) and allow it to cool a little while you make your sauce.

Set a heavy-bottomed frying pan (skillet) over a medium-high heat and add the oil. Once hot, add the onion and cook for about 5 minutes.

Next, stir in the ginger-garlic paste and green chilli. Cook for a minute, then add the garam masala, Sri Lankan curry powder, fresh tomatoes, passata and salt. Stir again and continue to cook until the sauce begins to bubble.

Next, carefully ladle in the cooked dal with its cooking liquid. Add the fresh coriander as you warm everything through to a simmer.

Drop in your butter (if using) before serving, then mix and swirl some fresh double cream on top for extra decadence. This isn't essential, but it is really tasty! Serve with chapatis or naan bread for dipping.

Gobi Manchurian

Serves 2

1 cauliflower, leaves removed, washed and cut into bite-sized florets
3 tbsp vegetable, sunflower or rapeseed (canola) oil
½ tbsp Sri Lankan Curry Powder (page 28)
1 tbsp Ginger-Garlic Paste (page 190)
1 red (bell) pepper, diced
4 spring onions (scallions), trimmed and sliced (keep the greens for garnish)

Sauce
3 tbsp dark soy sauce
3 tbsp ketchup
1 tbsp rice vinegar
¼ tsp Harissa (page 26)
½ tbsp honey
1 tbsp cornflour (cornstarch), mixed into 3 tbsp cold water
½ tsp Chinese Seven Spice (page 25)

To serve
Perfectly Fluffy Rice (page 189)
1 tbsp sesame seeds (optional)

Here, I am creating a twist on the traditional Manchurian – which is ordinarily cooked with a sauce made of soy and ketchup – by adding the spice blends. Growing up in Birmingham, we ate this loads of times at home because of the large Chinese community in the city. Mum learnt how to make it and my siblings and I asked her to make it every week.

It's so easy to make, ready in no time at all and tastes amazing, but a common criticism of this recipe when it is cooked traditionally, is how unhealthy it is to deep-fry the cauliflower. I've avoided this by baking the florets, which still creates a lovely crispy texture without the faff or extra calories!

This dish is equally lovely with paneer, tofu or chicken.

Preheat the oven to 200°C fan/220°C/425°F/gas mark 7 and line a baking tray (sheet) with baking paper.

Pat dry the cauliflower florets with paper towels then place in a bowl. Add 2 tablespoons of the oil and the Sri Lankan curry powder and mix thoroughly with your hands. Arrange on the lined tray. Roast for 20 minutes, checking and turning every 5 minutes. Cook until you start to get some colour.

Meanwhile, mix the ingredients for your sauce together in a bowl. Set aside.

Five minutes before the cauliflower is cooked, heat the remaining oil in a heavy-bottomed frying pan (skillet) and, when hot, add the ginger-garlic paste, red pepper and whites of the spring onions. Fry for 2 minutes, stirring continuously, then add your sauce. Continue to cook for a further 3 minutes until the sauce is bubbling. Add the cauliflower to the pan and continue to cook over a low heat while you prepare your rice.

Check your sauce for heat. If you want it spicier, add more harissa to taste.

Serve your sauce and veggies in a bowl piled over the rice. Scatter over the sesame seeds (if using) and the spring onion greens for garnish. Enjoy.

Fiery Jerk-inspired Pork

In this recipe, I use Scotch Bonnet chillies for a fiery pop, but you can calm it down with a less hot red or green chilli. This dish is lovely with our rainbow slaw, which has a cooling effect on your palate and gives a lovely crunch.

Add all the ingredients for the jerk sauce into a blender, turn to full power and blitz. You're looking for as smooth a paste as possible.

Rub the pork loin with half a cup of the blended sauce and leave to marinate for a few hours in the fridge.

When you are ready to cook, preheat your oven to 160°C fan/ 180°C/350°F/gas mark 4. Cook for 45-60 minutes, basting with a little more sauce every 15 minutes.

Serve with a bit more sauce to drizzle over and the slaw on the side.

750g (1lb 10oz) pork loin
Rainbow Slaw (page 196), to serve

Jerk sauce*
5 spring onions (scallions)
5 fresh thyme sprigs
2 tsp salt
1 tbsp brown sugar
2 Scotch Bonnet chillies
2 tbsp Jerk (page 27)
100ml (scant ½ cup) soy sauce
100g (3½oz) tomato ketchup
2 tbsp vegetable, sunflower or
   rapeseed (canola) oil
100ml (scant ½ cup) lime juice
   (about 3 or 4 limes)
3 garlic cloves
1 tbsp grated ginger

*This recipe makes more sauce than
   you need so keep the rest of it in the
   fridge or freezer for another time.

Ultimate (and Speedy) Butter Chicken

Butter chicken is often considered to be one of those dishes that takes ages to prepare and to cook, but this version will give you flavourful results in almost half the time with half the effort. Just allow your chicken to marinate overnight so that the meat is more succulent and the flavours can develop.

500g (1lb 2oz) boneless chicken breasts, cut into bite-size chunks
2 tbsp vegetable, sunflower or rapeseed (canola) oil
2 tbsp ghee
1 tbsp Tarka (page 28)
1 onion, sliced
2 tsp Ginger-Garlic Paste (page 190)
1 tbsp Garam Masala (page 26)
400g (14oz) can plum tomatoes
½ tsp Harissa (page 26)
1 tsp salt
50ml (3½ tbsp) double (heavy) cream
1 tsp sugar

Marinade
100g (scant ½ cup) Greek-style yoghurt
2 tbsp Ginger-Garlic Paste (page 190)
1 tbsp Garam Masala (page 26)
½ tsp Harissa (page 26)
1 tsp salt

To serve
Easy Midweek Naan (186)
300g (10½oz) Perfectly Fluffy Rice (page 189)
1 tbsp chopped fresh coriander (cilantro), optional

First make the marinade by combining all the ingredients in a large, non-metallic bowl. Add the chicken and give everything a good stir to combine. Cover and leave in the fridge overnight if you can, or for at least 2 hours to permeate the meat.

When you are ready to cook, heat the oil in a large, heavy-bottomed frying pan (skillet) over a medium heat. Add the chicken pieces with the marinade, and fry until browned, turning just once and resisting the urge to move them around the pan. They will need about 3 minutes on each side (you will finish cooking the chicken later in the sauce). Set aside.

Give the pan a quick wipe and put it back over the heat. Add the ghee and, when hot, add the tarka and allow the seeds to sizzle and pop for around 30 seconds, being careful not to burn. Next, add in your onion slices and stir to coat them in the spice-infused ghee. Cook gently for about 10 minutes, stirring regularly. Once the onions have started to sweat and become translucent, add in the ginger-garlic paste and cook for about a minute. When the raw smell has disappeared, add in the garam masala. Cook for a further 10 seconds, stirring to ensure nothing sticks to the bottom of the pan and burns.

Next, add the tomatoes, harissa and salt. Cook over a low-medium heat for 15 minutes. Turn off the heat and let the mixture cool a little, then, using a stick blender directly into the pan, carefully blend your sauce until it is completely smooth. If you're finding the sauce is splattering around too much, transfer it into a deeper pan for this step. You can also stir in a little water if the mixture is too thick.

Add the cream, sugar and chicken to the pan and give everything a good stir. Simmer for a further 10 minutes to ensure the chicken is thoroughly cooked. Serve with fresh naan bread, rice and chopped coriander scattered over the top.

Broad Bean, Tomato and Harissa Stew

This is a gorgeous one-pot plant-based stew that the vegetarians in your life are going to love you for. It's a dish you can make in advance and reheat on the day, and a great one for banging in the middle of the table with a big spoon and letting everyone dive in.

First, the fiddly bit! Skinning the broad beans takes a little time, but it is worth it. It turns a humble, slightly chewy bean into melt-in-the-mouth deliciousness. Some Asian shops sell frozen ones, already peeled, so grab some if you see them! You can obviously skip this step if you're using butter beans.

Put the beans in a bowl and pour over boiling water. When it is cool enough for you to get your hands in, gently squeeze the beans and they will pop out of their skins.

Next, heat 4 tablespoons of the oil in a frying pan (skillet) over a medium heat and cook the diced onions, stirring frequently, until they have softened and lightly caramelized. Add the garlic and sweat for a few minutes.

Add the tomatoes, tomato paste, honey and harissa. Cook for about 20 minutes until the oil separates. Stir, breaking up the tomatoes with the back of your spoon. You can add a little water if the mixture begins to stick.

Toss your beans in the remaining 2 tablespoons of oil and some black pepper, add the beans to the pan together with the coriander and red wine vinegar, and cook for a further 15 minutes.

Taste for salt, remembering that the dressing will add saltiness, so be sparing at this stage. You can always add more at the end.

Transfer to a serving dish and spread the tahini dressing out in the centre. Sprinkle with the za'atar and a few mint leaves, drizzle with some olive oil and enjoy with crusty bread.

700g (1lb 9oz) podded broad beans (fava beans) – fresh or frozen, or you could substitute canned butter beans (lima beans)
6 tbsp extra virgin olive oil, plus extra for drizzling
2 red onions, finely diced
2 garlic cloves, minced
400g (14oz) can plum tomatoes
2 tbsp tomato purée (paste)
2 tbsp honey
3 tsp Harissa (page 26)
Small bunch of fresh coriander (cilantro), chopped
5 tbsp red wine vinegar
Salt and freshly ground black pepper, to taste

To serve
Tahini Dressing (page 198)
2 tsp Za'atar (page 28)
Few sprigs of mint, leaves picked, roughly chopped
Fresh crusty bread

Serves 4

Tuna Steaks with Chimichurri

This dish is so lovely: healthy, vibrant and it also feels like a real treat. The chimichurri works so well, offering both flavour and moisture to the tuna, which can sometimes be quite a dry fish.

150g (5½oz) new potatoes
150g (5½oz) French beans (green beans), topped and tailed
2 tuna steaks (approx 140g/5oz each)
2 tbsp olive oil
3 tbsp capers
Salt and freshly ground black pepper,
Freshly made Chimichurri (page 199), to serve

Scrub the new potatoes clean and put them in a saucepan. Cover them in cold water and put them on to boil. Keep an eye on them while you prepare everything else; drain them after about 10 minutes or once a fork inserted meets little resistance.

Once the potatoes are ready, scoop them out of the simmering water. Season, then divide between two plates. Drop the beans into the simmering water in their place. Cook for 3 minutes, until bright and vibrant, then drain.

Brush the tuna steaks with 1 tablespoon of the oil, season with salt, then place in a dry, searingly hot frying pan (skillet). Cook for 2 minutes on each side, then remove from the pan. Add the other tablespoon of oil to the pan and, once hot, fry the capers until crisp.

Serve the tuna and beans alongside the potatoes, topped with plenty of chimichurri and finished with the capers.

Lamb-stuffed Aubergines with Feta and Pomegranate

It wasn't until I left home that I fell in love with aubergines. Mum used to hide them in my food when I was a kid because she wanted me to like them, but I always used to pick them out. Then, I discovered this dish and everything changed. Aubergines are now my go-to veg, whether it's for a quick curry or stuffing them with flavoured meat, as in this recipe. The key things here are to score the aubergines gently so you don't cut through the flesh, and not to scrimp on the toppings, as they will give you bundles of texture and flavour.

Preheat the oven to 190°C fan/210°C/410°F/gas mark 6½.

Arrange your aubergine halves on a baking tray (sheet). Drizzle over 2 tablespoons of the oil and season with the salt and pepper. Cover everything with foil and roast in the oven for about 35-40 minutes.

Meanwhile, add the remaining oil to a large heavy-bottomed frying pan (skillet) over a medium heat. Once the oil is hot, add the minced lamb. Cook while breaking down the mince with a wooden spoon - this should take about 6 minutes. You'll know it's done when all the pink has disappeared and you've got a lovely brown colour going on. Next, stir in the diced onion, ras el hanout and harissa. Cook for about 3-5 minutes, until your lamb is covered with the spices and the onions start to colour. Add your tomato purée. Turn down the heat, stir to combine and continue to cook for a further 2 minutes.

Once your aubergines are cooked, carefully scoop out the flesh from the inside. Add this to the pan and give everything another stir. Refill your hollowed-out aubergine skins with the lamb mixture and place them back on the tray and into the oven for a further 10 minutes.

While the stuffed aubergines are finishing off, toast the pine nuts gently in a small dry pan over a low heat.

Serve the aubergines with the crumbled feta, chopped mint and pine nuts. Finish with the beautiful pomegranate seeds. I also like to add some green salad leaves on the side with a further drizzle of olive oil.

Serves 4

4 aubergines (eggplants), cut in half lengthways and lightly scored on the diagonal
3 tbsp olive oil
½ tsp salt
½ tsp ground black pepper
500g (1lb 2oz) minced (ground) lamb
1 red onion, finely diced
2 tbsp Ras el Hanout (page 27)
1 tsp Harissa (page 26)
3 tbsp tomato purée (paste), or Big Batch Tomato Sauce (page 187) if you have some made

To serve
50g (1¾oz) pine nuts, lightly toasted
100g (3½oz) feta, crumbled
Handful of fresh mint leaves, roughly chopped
3 tbsp pomegranate seeds

Shashi's Crowd-pleasing Goan Fish/Vegetarian Curry

Mum went on holiday to Goa and tried this classic dish. She loved it, came home and created a vegetarian version for herself. When she makes this dish for the family, she cooks the sweet potatoes, takes a portion for herself out of the pan and then adds the fish for the rest of us. It's a great crowd-pleaser when you're cooking for vegans, veggies and people who eat fish.

The asparagus brings lovely texture and colour, without overpowering the flavour of the delicate fish. We tend to keep the skin on the fish as it helps to keep it intact, rather than flaking into the sauce, but if you can only find skinless, just go with what you have.

125g (4½oz) asparagus stalks, ends trimmed and peeled, tips chopped off the stalks

4 tbsp vegetable, sunflower or rapeseed (canola) oil

2 onions, sliced

2 green chillies, minced

2 tsp Ginger-Garlic Paste (page 190)

250g (9oz) fresh tomatoes, diced

2 x 400g (14oz) cans coconut milk

½ tsp salt, to taste

2 tsp Garam Masala (page 26)

½ tsp Harissa (page 26)

2 tbsp Sri Lankan Curry Powder (page 28)

1 sweet potato, peeled and diced

4 fillets white fish, whatever is your favourite, skin on and cut into 7.5cm (3in) chunks

1 tsp sugar, optional

Juice of ½ lime

2 tbsp freshly chopped coriander (cilantro)

Separate the asparagus tips and stalks into different bowls, as they will go into your pan at different stages of the cooking.

Add the oil to a heavy-bottomed frying pan (skillet) over a medium heat. When hot, add your sliced onions and cook until slightly browned, about 10 minutes. Then, add the green chillies and ginger-garlic paste and fry for a further minute until the raw smell from the garlic is gone.

Next, add the tomatoes and cook down until the oil starts to separate. Add a small amount of the coconut milk, then, using a hand-held stick blender in the pan, blend until smooth. If you're finding the sauce is splattering around too much you can transfer it into a deeper pan for this step and then back to the frying pan afterwards. You can also stir in a little water if the mixture is too thick.

Add the salt, garam masala, harissa, Sri Lankan curry powder and the rest of the coconut milk. Depending on how hot you like your dishes, you can add more or less harissa. Stir thoroughly to combine the flavours and break up any larger lumps of coconut milk.

Next, carefully add the sweet potato and asparagus stalks, put a lid on the pan and cook until the potatoes are nearly tender: check after 5 minutes. If you are separating out a vegetarian portion, now is the time to ladle it into a separate pan.

Add the fish and the asparagus tips to the main pan and cook for a further 3 minutes, until the fish is slightly flaking. If cooking a veggie portion, add half the asparagus tips to the veggie pan and the other half to the pan with the fish.

Check for seasoning and add more salt or Sri Lankan curry powder if you feel the dish needs it. Add the sugar at this point if using. Squeeze in the lime juice and give everything a good stir.

Serve with Perfectly Fluffy Rice (page 189) and the fresh coriander sprinkled on top.

Lu Ban Crispy Duck with Pancakes

Lu Ban is an award-winning Chinese restaurant in Liverpool. The Spice Kitchen team and I love going there and I was so happy when they said they would be up for cooking with our Chinese Seven Spice blend and developing a recipe for this book. I know you will love their take on classic crispy duck. Make sure you follow the instructions, especially the guidance to let the duck rest in the fridge for a few hours. This will guarantee you get that dried-out crispy texture we all know and love. This recipe suggests using mooli (daikon), which is a large white, radish. If you can't get this, then spring onions (scallions) or very thinly sliced regular radishes will work just as well.

Cooking the duck
2 large duck legs, skin on
500g (1lb 2oz) duck fat
100ml (scant ½ cup) Chinese Stock (page 191)

Duck rub
1 tbsp salt
1 tbsp soft brown sugar
1 tsp Chinese Seven Spice (page 25)

Seasonings
2 tsp Chinese Seven Spice (page 25)
1 tsp brown sugar
1 tsp smoked sea salt (or plain sea salt if that's what you have)

To serve
20 Chinese-style rice pancakes
6cm (2½in) chunk of cucumber, cut with a spiralizer or very finely julienned
4cm (1½in) chunk of mooli (daikon), cut with a spiralizer, or 8 spring onions (scallions) cut into ribbons
Hoisin sauce

Mix the ingredients for the duck rub in a bowl. Put the duck legs on a board and massage the duck rub evenly into the flesh. Cover and refrigerate for 2-3 hours. This will draw some of the moisture from the legs, which is what you want.

Preheat the oven to 140°C fan/160°C/325°F/gas mark 3.

Gently melt the duck fat in a wok or large frying pan (skillet).

Lay the duck legs in a small, deep-sided baking tin (pan), pour over the stock, then cover with the melted fat. Place in the oven and cook gently for 3-4 hours.

Remove from the oven and allow to cool in the fat, ideally overnight in a fridge. The stock and duck jelly will sink to the bottom of the tin.

Remove the legs, trim any excess skin and fat and tidy the bone (reserve the cooking fat to use another time).

Preheat the oven to 200°C fan/220°C/425°F/gas mark 7.

Place the duck on a baking tray (sheet) and cook for about 15 minutes until the skin becomes crispy. Allow to cool a little, then shred the skin and meat from the bones using two forks.

Put the seasonings in little separate bowls for sprinkling over the meat and serve with warm steamed pancakes, the cucumber, mooli or spring onions (or radish) and your favourite hoisin sauce.

Lamb Chops with Mango Chutney

Spice Freedom

This is such a fancy and impressive dinner, one that you can pull together in little more than 20 minutes. Lamb cutlets are so tender that you don't need to do much to them; they're lovely pink inside, but if you prefer them a little more well done, add a couple of minutes per side to the cooking time. Our Harissa, Garlic and Coriander Swirl Bread is brilliant with this but, if you're short on time, shop-bought flatbreads are just fine.

Put the chops on a board or plate and flatten them a little with your hands. Mix the tandoori masala with the oil and rub it all over the chops - meat and fat. Leave the chops for an hour if you have time; if not, leave them while you make the salsa.

Peel and dice both the mango and the avocado flesh. Dice the cherry tomatoes, strip the seeds and membrane from the pepper and dice it too. Put everything into a bowl and dress with the lime zest and juice, fish sauce, tandoori masala and salt. Add the coriander, give the salsa a stir and taste for seasoning.

Heat a dry frying pan (skillet) over a moderate-high heat. Cook the chops balanced on their layer of fat first, to render it; some will melt into the pan and help cook the rest of the cutlet. They'll take a couple of minutes on the fat, then a couple of minutes on each side.

Rest the chops for 5 minutes, then serve with the salsa and big hunks of bread.

Ready to experiment with your blends? This recipe is equally amazing with: **Mexican (Tex-Mex), Ras el Hanout, Jerk**

Serves 4

8 lamb cutlets (on the bone)
2 tbsp Tandoori Masala (page 27)
1 tbsp olive oil

Salsa
1 mango
1 avocado
150g (5½oz) cherry tomatoes
½ Romano or regular red (bell) pepper
Zest and juice of 1 lime
2 tsp fish sauce
2 tsp Tandoori Masala (page 27) (or use whatever Spice Freedom blend you've chosen for your lamb)
Pinch of salt, to taste
Handful of coriander (cilantro) leaves

To serve
Harissa, Garlic and Coriander Swirl Bread (page 96)

Sunday Lunch

Sunday remains the one day of the week where it's right and proper to spend hours in the kitchen cooking up a storm. With blended families, different dietary requirements and loads of recipes to try out, Sunday lunch is so much more than meat, veg and gravy! In this section, you'll also find ideas for spiced-up desserts, which I know will be your family favourites for years to come.

Whole Baked Cauliflower 4 Ways

Ready to experiment with your blends? This recipe is equally amazing with: Berbere, Tandoori Masala, Za'atar, Baharat

We love a whole baked cauliflower. It's easy to prepare and if you keep the leaves on (which are super-tasty), there's also no waste. In this recipe, we are giving you the freedom to choose how to spice your dish, with some serving suggestions to make a meal of it!

Preheat your oven to 180°C fan/200°C/400°F/gas mark 6 and line a baking tray (sheet) with baking paper.

Mix your chosen spice blend with the 60g (4 tablespoons) of melted butter, salt and 1 tablespoon of the olive oil."

Place the cauliflower on the lined tray and smear with the spiced butter mix. Use your hands to push the flavours into the crevices. Cook for 1-1½ hours, until the cauliflower is a rich brown and a knife inserted into the centre meets with no resistance, bearing in mind the cook time will vary with the size of your cauliflower.

20 minutes into the cooking time, carefully remove the pan from the oven and add the remaining butter and oil, and then baste your cauliflower every 15 minutes to keep it moist, like a roast chicken. Once the time is up, carve the cauliflower into portions, adding more seasoning if you feel the dish needs it.

Serving suggestions
Your baked cauliflower will work brilliantly as the main event in the centre of your table - you can serve it with a side of couscous or pitta for a more hearty meal.

If you've chosen the berbere blend, pair it with our lovely Spiced Tomato Chutney (page 196).

If you're opting for the tandoori masala, the flavours are great with our Zingy Mint and Coriander Chutney (page 198).

With the za'atar blend, we'd go for our Homemade Hummus (page 193), a squeeze of lemon juice and some Pickled Red Onions (page 195).

Going down the baharat route? Throw over some pomegranate seeds and serve with our Garlic Yoghurt (page 193).

Serves 2

60g (4 tbsp) salted butter, melted gently in a pan, plus 2 tbsp for basting
Generous pinch of salt
2 tbsp olive oil
1 whole cauliflower, leaves included

Spice suggestions
Choose from:
1 tbsp Berbere (page 25)
1 tbsp Tandoori Masala (page 27)
1 tbsp Za'atar (page 28)
1 tbsp Baharat (page 25)

Lamb and Apricot Tagine

Serves 4–6

This much-loved stew is a favourite in my home. The slow-cooked lamb literally melts in your mouth. Be sure to follow the guidelines and marinate overnight. Trust me: it's worth it.

In a bowl, mix 2 tablespoons of the olive oil with half the ras el hanout and half of the harissa, along with two of the crushed garlic cloves. Massage into the lamb, cover and leave in the fridge overnight.

When you are ready to cook, preheat the oven to 160°C fan/ 180°C/350°F/gas mark 4.

Heat a heavy-bottomed frying pan (skillet) until smoking hot, then drizzle in your remaining oil. Carefully add the marinated lamb and brown all over. One minute before your lamb is done, add the remaining garlic and fry gently for 20 seconds, being careful not to burn. Transfer your lamb and garlic to a heavy, lidded ovenproof casserole and add the apricots, the remaining ras el hanout and harissa, the saffron if using, stock, onions, tomatoes, honey, thyme and salt.

Cook the tagine with the lid on for 2–3 hours, until the lamb is falling apart.

Once cooked, remove from the oven and check the consistency of the sauce. If it's too watery, remove the lamb and reduce the sauce on the hob until it has thickened.

Serve garnished with chopped coriander, mint and a nice heap of couscous, if you like.

4 tbsp olive oil
2 tbsp Ras el Hanout (page 27)
1 tsp Harissa (page 26)
6 garlic cloves, crushed
800g (1lb 12oz) boneless lamb
  shoulder, diced
150g (5½oz) dried apricots
Large pinch of saffron (optional)
600ml (generous 2½ cups) chicken
  stock (bouillon) or water
2 onions, roughly chopped
2 x 400g (14oz) cans chopped
  tomatoes
1 tbsp honey
A few thyme sprigs
Salt, to taste

To serve
Handful of coriander (cilantro),
  chopped
Handful of mint leaves, chopped

Lamb Raan with Super-spiced Spuds

Lamb
Half leg of lamb (roughly 1kg/2lb 4oz)
1 garlic clove, thinly sliced
2 tsp Ginger-Garlic Paste (page 190)
250g (1¼ cups) Greek-style yoghurt
1 onion, roughly chopped
1 tbsp Garam Masala (page 26)
1 tbsp Tandoori Masala (page 27)
½ tsp Harissa (page 26) (optional)
Handful of fresh mint leaves
Juice of 1 lemon (or 2 limes if you
   have them)
1 tsp salt
6 shallots, peeled but left whole

Super-spiced spuds
500g (1lb 2oz) baby potatoes, skin on
   and halved (you can use canned if
   you have them)
40g (3 tbsp) butter
3 tbsp vegetable, sunflower or
   rapeseed (canola) oil
6 spring onions (scallions), trimmed
   and sliced
Juice of ½ lime
1 tsp Sri Lankan Curry Powder
   (page 28)
½ tsp salt
Freshly ground black pepper, to taste

To serve
Pickled Red Onions (page 195)
Bunch of coriander (cilantro),
   roughly chopped

This is a dish you'll need to prepare three days before you want to eat it, but trust me, it's worth it. It's a total showstopper for Sunday lunch and a perfect alternative to the traditional roast. In my home, we've cooked lamb raan for Christmas dinner when the family has come over and it's always gone down a storm – and for good reason. The flavour profile is deep, but has a nice citrussy balance because of the lemon, yoghurt and tandoori.

Many recipes you'll see call for a whole leg of lamb, but we've created this recipe for half a leg of lamb and this is still a lot of meat for 4 people. Serve simply with super-spiced spuds!

Poke holes into the lamb with a sharp knife and push your garlic slices into the holes.

Put the ginger-garlic paste, yoghurt, onion, garam masala, tandoori masala, harissa (if using), mint, lemon juice and salt into your blender. Blitz to form a paste.

Rub the paste all over the lamb with your hands, massaging it into the cuts. Place into a large zip-lock freezer bag, seal and put it in the fridge for 2-3 days.

When you are ready to get cooking, preheat the oven to 170°C fan/190°C/375°F/gas mark 5.

Put the lamb and all the marinade into a roasting tin (pan). Cover with foil and cook for 2½ hours. If you like your lamb well done, you can cook it for 3 hours.

This step is really important. Set a timer and baste the lamb every 20-25 minutes to keep your meat moist. You will notice each time you take it out to baste, the marinade will have cooked down more and more. Eventually, the marinade will start to stick to the base of the tin, at this point add in about 3 tablespoons of water.

Forty-five minutes before the cook time is up, add the shallots to the roasting tin and give everything a stir. This is also the time to prepare your spuds. Unless you are using canned, cook the new potatoes for 10 minutes in a saucepan of boiling

water with a good pinch of salt. Drain then let them steam-dry in a colander for 5 minutes.

Put the potatoes into a separate roasting tin with the butter, oil, spring onions, lime juice, Sri Lankan curry powder, salt and pepper. Give everything a good stir and pop the tin into the oven with the lamb to let the potatoes cook and crisp up. When you put the potatoes into the oven, take the foil off the lamb, give it another good baste (and a little more water if needed) to let the top of the meat brown for the remainder of the cook time.

Take out the lamb, cover with foil and let it rest for 15 minutes. Turn up the oven to high, give the

potatoes a stir and let them continue to crisp up in the oven while the lamb rests.

Transfer the lamb to a platter, scatter with some of the Pickled Red Onions and carve the meat at the table. Serve the potatoes in a separate dish, sprinkled with the coriander. Let everyone dive in and enjoy.

*Top tip: Carve any lamb that's left over after you've eaten and add it to the remaining marinade sauce for an amazing leftover meal. You can add a little water, yoghurt or cream to create more sauce. Serve with rice or bread. A total bonus.

147

Tandoori Spiced Celeriac and Butternut Squash Pie

This is a lovely, warming pie for autumn. Keep everything nice and chunky below the crisp top, or you risk ending up with vegetable mush. This will also work beautifully with carrots, parsnips or a swede (rutabaga) – any dense root vegetable or a different squash would be equally delicious.

1 celeriac (celery root)
1 small butternut squash
2 leeks, washed and trimmed
Large pinch of salt
2 tbsp olive oil
2 tbsp Tandoori Masala (page 27)
60g (4 tbsp) butter
60g (2¼oz) plain (all-purpose) flour
600ml (generous 2½ cups) vegetable stock (bouillon)

Topping
150g (½ cup plus 2½ tbsp) butter
1 x 250g (9oz) packet filo (phyllo) pastry sheets
2 tbsp black onion seeds

To prepare the filling, peel the celeriac and squash. Cut into chunks: it's hard, with round vegetables, but aim for cubes about 2cm (¾in) along each edge. Slice the leeks into 1cm (½in) rounds.

Preheat the oven to 200°C fan/220°C/425°F/gas mark 7. Spread everything over a baking tin (pan), in a single layer if you can manage it. Dress with the salt, olive oil and 1 tablespoon of the tandoori blend. Toss so that all the veg is covered and roast in the oven for 20 minutes. The veg will be going into the oven again later, so don't overcook it in the early stages, or you're going to end up with a mush.

Melt the butter in a large saucepan and add the flour. Stir through and cook for at least 2 minutes over a gentle heat. Add the remaining tablespoon of spice blend, then whisk in a splash of the stock. Keep adding the stock bit by bit, until you have a smooth sauce. Reduce until thick enough to coat the back of your spoon, then stir through the roasted vegetables. Tip into a roasting dish. Set the filling aside to cool while you prepare the topping.

Melt the butter in a small saucepan. Use a pastry brush to paint butter all over a sheet of filo, keeping the rest covered with a damp dish towel (filo dries out really fast). Scrunch the sheet up by pulling it in with your fingertips to create ridges, peaks and valleys in it. Place in a corner of the dish over the pie filling. Repeat with more sheets of filo, until the entire surface is covered. Top with the black onion seeds.

Bake at 200°C fan/220°C/425°F/gas mark 7 for 30 minutes, until crisp and golden brown on top. Allow to cool for 5 minutes before serving.

Staff Chicken Curry

Serves 4

The team at Spice Kitchen is awesome; we sit and eat lunch together every day and take turns to cook for one another. This recipe is one of our favourites. I make up a big batch in an evening and take it in for us to share.

You can make this belter in advance for friends coming round for dinner. It's the perfect go-to, no-fuss curry that's totally banging: everyone will love you for it!

10–12 skinless, boneless chicken thighs
500ml (2 cups) Tarka Sauce (page 188)
2 tbsp vegetable, sunflower or
  rapeseed (canola) oil
Handful of coriander (cilantro),
  chopped, to serve

Marinade
Juice of 1 lemon
3 tbsp Greek-style yoghurt, plus extra
  to serve
1 tsp Tandoori Masala (page 27)
2 tsp Ginger-Garlic Paste (page 190)

Optional
Salt, to taste
1 tsp Garam Masala (page 26)

Put the marinade ingredients into a large bowl. Cut the chicken into large chunks and add to the marinade. Stir to combine, cover and leave in the fridge for 3 hours, but preferably overnight.

When you are ready to cook, add the tarka sauce to a large saucepan and slowly bring to a simmer.

Meanwhile, set a large, heavy-bottomed frying pan (skillet) over a medium-high heat. Add the oil and, once hot, gently add your chicken into the pan. Fry for 2-3 minutes on each side until the meat starts to take on colour. Only turn once, resisting the urge to keep moving the chicken in the pan; just let it cook and seal.

Next, carefully stir the chicken into the sauce. Return to a very gentle simmer and cook like that for 10 minutes, or until the chicken is thoroughly cooked through. (You can take out one piece to check). The sauce will naturally thicken, so add a little water if you prefer a thinner consistency.

Taste and adjust the seasoning by adding salt if you think your curry needs it. You can also add a little garam masala at this stage if you think the sauce needs an extra boost of flavour.

Serve with rice or naan, fresh coriander and a heap of yoghurt on the side.

Beef Meatballs with Baharat and Prunes

These meatballs are great served simply with a crisp salad, but they really come into their own with this sauce, served in generous portions over couscous. Perfect for cold winter nights.

To make the meatballs, mix the prunes with the minced beef, baharat blend, oil and salt. Fry off a little pinch of the mix, taste for seasoning and adjust the spice or salt as needed, then put the meat aside so the flavours can develop.

Meanwhile, prepare the sauce. Fry the onion in 1 tablespoon of the oil over a moderate heat, until the onion has softened but not taken on any colour. Add the garlic and fry for a couple of minutes.

Stir the baharat through the onion and garlic. Add the honey and stock and bring to a gentle simmer. Reduce by half.

While your sauce simmers away, form the seasoned meat into balls the size of ping-pong balls. Fry in a dry, non-stick frying pan (skillet) until caramelized on the outside and cooked all the way through (break one open to check). Make sure you move the meatballs around a little, or they will burn on one side and stay raw on the other.

Meanwhile, cook your couscous according to the packet instructions.

Add the halved prunes to the reduced sauce along with the cooked meatballs and the final tablespoon of olive oil. Allow everything to bubble away together for 5 minutes before topping with the herbs and serving over the couscous.

Serves 4

75g (2½oz) pitted prunes, finely diced
400g (14oz) minced (ground) beef
5 tsp Baharat (page 25)
1 tbsp olive oil
Large pinch of salt

Sauce
2 medium onions, finely diced
2 tbsp olive oil
3 garlic cloves, minced
1 tbsp Baharat (page 25)
2 tbsp honey
500ml (2 cups) beef stock (bouillon)
100g (3½oz) pitted prunes, halved

To serve
250g (9oz) couscous
Handful of coriander (cilantro) leaves
Handful of fresh parsley leaves

Sticky Ribs and
Stir-fried Greens

You'll need to prepare the ribs the night before you want to eat; the marinating time is really important here to ensure the ribs are really tender and rich in flavour. Serve this with some Perfectly Fluffy Rice (page 189).

Ribs

500g (1lb 2oz) pork ribs, separated into individual lengths
3 tbsp soy sauce
1 tbsp Chinese Seven Spice (page 25)
Large pinch of salt
3 spring onions (scallions), trimmed and left whole
40g (1¼oz) fresh ginger, peeled and roughly chopped
2 tbsp Shaoxing wine
1 tbsp rice vinegar
5 tbsp dark brown sugar

Stir-fried greens

2 tbsp sesame oil
2 garlic cloves, finely sliced
300g (10½oz) greens, such as choy sum or pak choi (bok choy), leaves separated
1 tbsp soy sauce
2 tsp rice vinegar
2 tsp oyster sauce
1 tbsp sesame seeds

Toss the ribs in the soy sauce, Chinese seven spice and salt. Cover and leave to marinate in the fridge overnight.

The next day, put the ribs and their marinating liquid in a saucepan along with the spring onions and ginger. Cover with water, put a lid on, bring to a simmer and cook for 1½ hours until the meat is tender and starting to pull away from the bone.

Remove the ribs from the pan (don't throw the stock away!) and place on a baking tray (sheet) lined with baking paper.

Bring the stock to a rolling boil and reduce by half. Add the Shaoxing wine, vinegar and sugar. Continue to reduce the sauce until sticky.

Preheat the oven to 220°C fan/240°C/475°F/gas mark 9. Generously coat the ribs with the sticky sauce and cook for 10 minutes until burnished and caramelized.

Meanwhile, stir-fry the greens. Heat 1 tablespoon of the sesame oil in a wok or wide saucepan over a high heat and add the garlic. Fry for 15 seconds, or until just starting to turn golden, then add the greens. Keep them moving for a couple of minutes, then add the soy sauce, rice vinegar, oyster sauce and the second tablespoon of sesame oil. Turn off the heat and add the sesame seeds.

Brush the hot ribs with a little more sauce before serving with the greens and some rice.

Za'atar Lamb Koftes with Pickled Red Onions

Koftes
500g (1lb 2oz) minced (ground) lamb
2 tbsp Za'atar (page 28)
3 garlic cloves, minced
Handful of mint leaves, finely chopped
½ tsp salt
½ tsp Harissa (page 26), optional

1 tsp vegetable, sunflower or rapeseed (canola) oil, for greasing

To serve
4 pitta breads
2 tbsp Pickled Red Onions (page 195)
¼ Iceberg lettuce, finely shredded
¼ cucumber, grated
Freshly chopped green or red chillies (optional)
2 tbsp Za'atar Yoghurt (page 195)
Juice of 1 lemon

I love the versatility of this spiced-up kofte mixture. It makes awesome koftes, but by simply changing their shape you can make equally banging lamb burgers!

Soak 12 bamboo skewers in water for 30 minutes.

To make the koftes, thoroughly mix together all the ingredients for the koftes in a large bowl, kneading with your hands for a blended consistency. (You can fry a small amount of the mixture in some oil to taste and check the seasoning and add more if you think it needs extra.)

Lightly grease a baking tray (sheet) with the oil.

Next, working with wet hands, divide your kofte mixture evenly into 12 portions and shape into sausage or log shapes. Line up on your baking tray. Leave to chill in the fridge for an hour.

When you're ready to cook, preheat your oven to 220°C fan/ 240°C/475°F/gas mark 9. Cook for 12-15 minutes, or until the lamb is no longer pink inside and is a lovely sizzling brown on the outside. Leave to rest for 5 minutes.

Meanwhile, warm the pitta breads under your grill (broiler) according to the packet instructions. Plate up with the koftes on top, and pile high with the pickled onions, salad and yoghurt dressing. Finish with a squeeze of lemon juice and serve immediately.

Bunny Chow

50ml (3½ tbsp) vegetable, sunflower or rapeseed (canola) oil

1 large onion, finely diced

2 medium potatoes, peeled, washed and diced

1 green chilli, seeds and membrane removed, minced

2 tbsp Ginger-Garlic Paste (page 190)

1 tsp Garam Masala (page 26)

1 tsp Sri Lankan Curry Powder (page 28)

2 large tomatoes, diced

½ tsp sugar (optional but it balances the dish well)

400g (14oz) can butter beans (lima beans), drained and rinsed

100ml (scant ½ cup) passata (strained tomatoes)

100ml (scant ½ cup) water

Handful of spinach, fresh or frozen (optional but it really elevates the dish)

2 tbsp roughly chopped coriander (cilantro), plus a little to serve

Salt and freshly ground black pepper, to taste

To serve

4 crusty white bread rolls

2 tbsp Tamarind Chutney (page 197) (optional)

This South African street food is essentially a humble curry served in a bread roll... but don't be fooled, it's SO much more than that. It's one of the region of Durban's most popular dishes, and for good reason. Bunny chow has a rich cultural backstory and although no one is entirely sure of its exact origin, the story goes that migrant workers had no way of carrying their lunch to work, so they stored it inside a bread roll until it was time to eat.

Preheat the oven to 180°C fan/200°C/400°F/gas mark 6.

First prepare the bread rolls. Slice off the tops and reserve them. Carefully, scoop out the soft interior from the rolls* to make a cavity, without going right to the base: you want the buns intact with no holes for the curry to fall through. Place the tops back on the hollowed-out buns and arrange them on a baking sheet. Set aside.

Heat the oil in a heavy-bottomed frying pan (skillet) over a medium heat. Once hot, add the diced onion, potato and chilli. Fry gently for about 8 minutes, until the veg have softened and taken on some colour. As the starch comes out of the potatoes they may start to catch on the bottom of the pan. This is fine and will add flavour when you add the passata and water. Just keep stirring so the mixture doesn't burn.

Next, add in the ginger-garlic paste and cook for a further minute, again stirring regularly so the mixture doesn't burn.

Now it's time to get your bread rolls into the oven. They need 6-8 minutes to lightly brown and cook through, so you might want to set a timer to ensure they don't overcook or burn.

Meanwhile, stir the garam masala and Sri Lankan curry powder, diced tomatoes, sugar (if using) and some salt and pepper into the pan with the onions and potatoes. Cook for a further 3 minutes, stirring regularly.

Next, add in your butter beans, passata and water. Simmer for 5-8 minutes until they are fully heated. Check that your potatoes are soft and, if they need a bit longer, cook for a further 2-3 minutes. This is also the time to add your spinach (if using).

Turn off the heat and add the fresh coriander. Stir to combine.

Take your bread rolls out of the oven and carefully fill them with your lovely veggie mixture.

Drizzle over the tamarind chutney (if using) and sprinkle with more coriander. Pop the lids back on and serve immediately.

*Top tip: Use the scooped out interiors from the bread rolls to make breadcrumbs.

Harissa-spiced Veggie Lasagne

Serves 4–6

This is a lasagne for when you have a little spare time to get the tunes on, don your apron and cook up a storm. It makes enough for a good meal with leftovers for the next day. For a vegan-friendly version, replace the butter, milk, Cheddar and Parmesan with plant-based alternatives.

Gently warm the tomato sauce in a large saucepan. When it comes up to heat, set aside.

To make the pesto, simply put all the ingredients in a blender and blitz until smooth. You can add a splash of water if you need to loosen things up a bit.

Heat the oil in a large frying pan, add the onion, and fry for a couple of minutes until softened. Add the red peppers, mushrooms, courgette, aubergine, harissa, salt and pepper. Cook over a medium-high heat, stirring regularly, for about 10 minutes or until the veggies take on some colour. Stir in the pesto and mix thoroughly. Set aside.

For the cheese sauce, pour the milk into a large saucepan and add the flour and butter. Set over a medium heat and begin to whisk. As the milk warms through, the butter will melt and the flour will disappear. Keep whisking as everything combines and thickens. Once it starts to bubble, add the cheese. Once it has melted turn off the heat and set the pan aside.

Preheat the oven to 190°C fan/210°C/410°F/gas mark 6½ and grab a large ovenproof baking dish: it's time to build your lasagne! Start with half the pesto-veggie mix, then half the tomato sauce, followed by a layer of lasagne sheets. Top with half the cheese sauce and repeat, finishing with a final layer of lasagne sheets and the other half of the cheese sauce on the top. Arrange the sliced tomatoes and shake over the Parmesan and Italian seasoning.

Cover with foil and bake in the oven for 30 minutes. After the cooking time is up, take off the foil and return the dish to the oven for a final 10 minutes to get the cheesy topping bubbling and brown. Place on the middle of your table with a big spoon so that everyone can dive in. Serve with a green salad and garlic bread or Coriander Swirl Bread.

800g (1lb 12oz) Big Batch Tomato Sauce (page 187)
2 tbsp vegetable, sunflower or rapeseed (canola) oil
1 red onion, peeled, halved and cut into half moons
2 red (bell) peppers, tops removed, deseeded and sliced
250g (9oz) mushrooms, chopped
1 courgette (zucchini), diced
1 aubergine (eggplant), diced
½ tsp Harissa (page 26)
½ tsp salt
½ tsp freshly ground black pepper
8–10 lasagne sheets (or more, depending on the size of your dish)

Pesto
75g (5½oz) shelled pistachio nuts
30g (2¼oz) basil leaves and stems, roughly chopped
2 tbsp olive oil
20g (¾oz) Parmesan cheese, grated
Zest of 1 lemon and juice of ½
½ tsp salt

Cheese sauce
300ml (1¼ cups) milk
2 tbsp plain (all-purpose) flour
50g (3½ tbsp) butter
150g (5½oz) mature Cheddar cheese

Topping
1 big tomato, thinly sliced
4 tbsp grated Parmesan cheese (or firm mozzarella if you have some)
½ tsp Italian Seasoning (page 26)

To serve
Garlic bread or, if you have time to bake, Harissa, Garlic and Coriander Swirl Bread (page 96)

Spiced Mango
Ice Cream

Makes just over 1 litre (4⅓ cups)

600g (1lb 5oz) mango pulp
400ml (1¾ cups) sweetened
   condensed milk
300ml (1¼ cups) crème fraîche
Juice of 1 lime
2 tsp Harissa (page 26), or to taste

No-churn ice cream is a breeze: no custard, no ice-cream machine, just a quick whisk and freeze. The heat and warmth of harissa is great with mango.

Whisk together the mango pulp and condensed milk then fold through the crème fraîche and lime juice.

Add the harissa gradually, starting with a small pinch, and taste once you've stirred the mixture together until the flavour is as you like it. Pour into a freezerproof container and freeze for at least 4 hours, or until solid. Allow to soften out of the freezer for 5 minutes before scooping.

Eton Mess with Strawberries and Black Pepper

Even if the weather lets you down, the flavours of this spiced-up summer treat never will. We bring to you a warming twist on a British classic.

Put half the strawberries in a saucepan with 4 tablespoons of the sugar. Squash them a little and place over a low heat. Add the whole peppercorns and simmer until the strawberries have collapsed (keep an eye on them, as you don't want the sugar to turn into caramel). Squash completely, pour through a sieve (strainer) and set aside to cool.

Meanwhile, slice the remaining strawberries into quarters and put in a bowl. Cover with the rest of the sugar and a good grinding of black pepper. Toss and set aside. Whip the cream to soft peaks and crumble the meringues.

Gently ribbon the strawberry sauce through the cream, then fold through the sliced strawberries and meringue pieces. Serve immediately.

500g (1lb 5oz) strawberries, hulled
6 tbsp caster (superfine) sugar
1 tbsp whole black peppercorns
Freshly ground black pepper
300ml (1¼ cups) double (heavy) cream
6 shop-bought meringue nests

Serves 6

Gingerbread and Peanut Brownies

250g (1 cup plus 2 tbsp) unsalted
   butter, cut into cubes, plus extra
   for greasing
300g (10½oz) dark (bittersweet)
   chocolate, roughly chopped
1 tbsp Gingerbread blend (page 26)
300g (10½oz) caster (superfine) sugar
4 eggs
80g (2¾oz) peanuts
60g (2¼oz) plain (all-purpose) flour
60g (2¼oz) cocoa powder
   (unsweetened cocoa)
½ tsp baking powder
Generous pinch of sea salt

The only thing in this world I can think of that's better than a chocolate brownie is a gingerbread chocolate brownie. Make these, hide them from your friends and family and don't ever share!

Preheat your oven to 140°C fan/160°C/320°F/gas mark 3. Butter and line a 25cm (10in) square cake tin (cake pan). Use plenty of paper to make it easy to pull the brownies out; they will be too fudgy and delicate to lift out of the tin.

Melt the butter with 200g (7oz) of the chocolate, either in a heatproof bowl set over a pan of gently simmering water or in short blasts in the microwave. Once melted, whisk in the gingerbread blend and sugar until smooth. Crack in the eggs, one at a time, and beat to combine.

Dry-toast the peanuts in a frying pan (skillet) until golden, then chop roughly.

Sift together the flour, cocoa and baking powder and stir through the batter. Fold in the rest of the chopped chocolate and the peanuts.

Bake for 40-45 minutes, until a skewer inserted comes out sticky, but with no raw batter attached. Sprinkle with a good pinch of sea salt and leave to cool completely before cutting into squares.

Drinks and Snacks

'Spice blends in drinks?' I imagine you're wondering. You bet. There are so many creative and delicious ways to use your blends, and so if you're ready for some experimentation, then you're going to want to try out some of these beauties. I've got something for every occasion - winter warmers, summer coolers, dinner party drinks and, of course, the legendary masala chai for a morning treat. And, for those of you who like a little snack with your tipple, there are a few spiced-up options for you to choose from!

Easy Masala Chai

Behold the dreamy chai. Warming, creamy, packed with natural sweetness and, of course, perfectly spiced! In India, brewing chai is considered an artform, but we want you to be able to make it just as easily at home, so here is a recipe that will elevate you to the status of artist! The spices in this blend here are kept whole so they can be easily removed.

Masala Chai blend

1g ginger powder (you can also use a thin slice of fresh ginger if you have some)
2g cardamom pods
2g cinnamon bark
1g whole cloves
2g fennel seeds
1g whole black peppercorns
1g nutmeg

For the chai

400ml (1¾ cups) water
2 black tea bags (regular or Assam is fine)
1 batch Masala Chai blend (see above)
250ml (generous 1 cup) your favourite milk (whole milk, cashew or oat work equally well)
Sugar or maple syrup, depending on your preference

Lightly bash your spices using a pestle and mortar.

Bring the water to a rolling boil in a saucepan over a medium-high heat, then add the tea bags and your masala chai blend. Turn off the heat and allow to brew for around 10 minutes, making sure you stir occasionally. (Letting the chai brew for longer gives a stronger, creamier flavour, so if you like your chai with a punch, don't rush this step.)

Add the milk and bring the chai back to a simmer - make sure your pan doesn't bubble over.

Turn off the heat and add sugar or maple syrup to taste. We tend to add around 1-2 teaspoons per serving. Strain and then ladle your chai into pre-warmed mugs. Enjoy immediately.

Chai Syrup

This syrup forms the base of the Chai Lassi, Chaitini and Chai Latte recipes that follow. It's so easy to make and worth taking the time to let the flavours really mingle together during the steeping process.

Makes enough for 8 shots

13g Masala Chai blend (page 170)
250ml (generous 1 cup) water
45g (1½oz) sugar

Combine the ingredients in a heavy-bottomed saucepan over a medium heat. Simmer until the sugar is dissolved and the spices start to smell fragrant (about 3-5 minutes).

Remove the heat and let the spices steep in the liquid for about 20 minutes (a more intense flavour will develop the longer it is steeped).

Fine strain (best through a funnel lined with filter paper) into a clean glass bottle or jar and refrigerate to chill. Use as needed in the chai-based drinks recipes in this chapter.

Chai Lassi

Our take on this famous north Indian classic. Yoghurt infused with gorgeous chai spices. Say. No. More.

Makes 2 drinks

10 ice cubes
80ml (⅓ cup) milk (dairy or oat milk work equally well)
150g (¾ cup) Greek-style yoghurt
Pinch of salt
50ml (3½ tbsp) Chai Syrup (see left)

Add your ice cubes, milk, yoghurt, salt and chai syrup to a blender. Blitz until really smooth.

Serve immediately.

Variation
Add 100g (3½oz) frozen mango to easily pimp up this recipe... and you'll have a vibrant chai and mango lassi.

Chaitini

I love serving this drink as the summer changes into autumn. It's such a perfect way to celebrate the changing of the seasons as our bodies start to crave more warming, comforting drinks rather than the heady fizz of summer. This recipe makes enough for one but is easy to scale up if you're making it for guests.

Makes 1 drink

1½ shots (4½ tbsp) vanilla vodka
½ shot (1½ tbsp) coffee liqueur
1 shot (3 tbsp) Chai Syrup (see opposite)
50ml (3½ tbsp) whole milk/oat milk, whichever you prefer

To serve (optional)
1 cracked cardamom pod
1 star anise

Shake the ingredients in a cocktail shaker over plenty of ice. Strain into a V-shaped cocktail glass. Garnish with the cracked cardamom pod and star anise, if using.

Serve immediately.

Chai Latte

This fragrant latte is a great winter warmer. I love to make it on a cold morning. It makes me think of Christmas, but you should enjoy it anytime during the year!

Makes 1 drink

300ml (1¼ cups) your favourite milk, plus a little extra for frothing
3–4 tbsp Chai Syrup (see opposite)

Warm your milk slowly in a non-stick saucepan, being careful not to let it bubble over.

Add your chai syrup to a mug and carefully pour in the hot milk. Stir to combine.

If you have a milk frother, foam your remaining milk and pour into your mug. If not, you can pour the milk into a large jar with a lid. Screw the lid on and then shake the jar until your milk is lovely and frothy - this normally takes about 1 minute.

Enjoy immediately.

Gingerbread Hot Chocolate

We all know that there aren't many things in this world more sublime than good-quality hot chocolate. The addition of gingerbread to this recipe takes it to the next level.

Serves 2

45g (1¾oz) your favourite cocoa powder (unsweetened cocoa)
2 tbsp Gingerbread blend (page 26)
1–2 tbsp sugar or maple syrup
Tiny pinch of salt
600ml (generous 2½ cups) milk, dairy or plant-based (or just use your mug as a measure)

Whisk together the cocoa, gingerbread blend, sugar or syrup, salt and a good splash of the milk in a non-stick saucepan. Add the rest of the milk and warm gently over a medium heat until hot.

For a frothy finish you can whizz up the mixture using a hand-held blender but do be careful not to let it splash over you. Pour into mugs and enjoy immediately.

Cosy Gingerbread Latte

This warming drink is like getting a hug from your mug. I love to make it on an early autumn evening when we are outdoors with the fire pit roaring.

Serves 2

500ml (2 cups) milk, dairy or plant-based
2 tsp Gingerbread blend (page 26), plus extra, to finish
2 tbsp sugar
½ tsp vanilla extract
2 shots (6 tbsp) espresso
Whipped cream, to serve (optional)

Heat a little of the milk in a non-stick saucepan, then gently add the gingerbread blend. Stir thoroughly to combine and add the sugar and vanilla extract.

Pour in the rest of the milk, stirring regularly. Heat gently until hot - remove from the heat before your latte starts to boil.

Meanwhile, add an espresso shot to the bottom of each mug. Gently pour in your hot spiced milk, then squirt on some whipped cream, if you like. Finish with a final dusting of gingerbread blend.

Apricot and Harissa Bellini

I love these Bellinis on a hot summer's day; they're great for a party or celebration and a real show-stopper. The apricot purée needs to chill so plan ahead and get that made first. The purée ingredients will make enough for 10 Bellinis, and a bottle of Prosecco will give you five, so with my logic it makes total sense to buy two bottles of Prosecco and use the lot!!

Makes 5 drinks, with enough purée for another 5

1 bottle (75cl) Prosecco
Dried rose petals, to garnish

Apricot purée
45g (1¾oz) sugar
5 tbsp water
½ tsp Harissa (page 26)
200g (7oz) ripe apricots, pitted and chopped

First make the purée. Combine the sugar, water and harissa blend in a heavy-bottomed saucepan. Heat gently and simmer for 3-5 minutes until the sugar is dissolved. Remove from the heat and let everything steep in the liquid for about 15 minutes.

Add the chopped apricots to a blender, then fine strain (best through a funnel lined with filter paper) the harissa-spiced syrup directly into the apricots. Blend on high until completely smooth. Transfer to a container, cover and refrigerate until completely chilled.

To serve your Bellinis, slowly fill your glasses with Prosecco then carefully spoon 2 tablespoons of the apricot purée into each one. Stirring takes away the clarity of the drink but you'll really taste the lovely flavours this way.

Garnish with a sprinkle of dried rose petals.

Indian-inspired Cooler

Sweet, tangy and fizzy. What's not to love? This is the perfect cooling drink when it's hot outside. It's also great to serve on trays when guests come. The recipe here makes one drink but the ingredients are easy to scale up for as many as you need.

Makes 1 drink

50g (1¾oz) frozen or fresh mango*
Juice of 1 lime
Scant 4 tbsp Chai Syrup (page 172)
Ice cubes
Sparkling water (enough to top up your glasses)

To garnish
Wedge of lime
Star anise (optional)

Place the mango, lime juice and chai syrup into your blender and blitz until completely smooth.

Pour the blend into a tall glass filled with ice cubes and top up with sparkling water. Stir until combined and serve garnished with a wedge of lime and a star anise if using.

*If using fresh mango rather than frozen, add a handful of ice to the blender.

Baharat-roasted Chickpeas

A delicious, warming snack that's super-easy and offers a great alternative for people who don't like or can't eat nuts. Also perfect for those occasions when you look in the cupboard and all that's there is a lonely can of chickpeas!

Makes enough for 2–4 as a snack

1 tbsp Baharat (page 25)
½ tsp salt
2 tbsp vegetable oil
400g (14oz) can chickpeas (garbanzo beans), rinsed and drained

Preheat the oven to 180°C fan/200°C/400°F/ gas mark 6 and line a baking (cookie) sheet with baking paper.

Mix your baharat in a bowl with the salt and the oil.

Dry the rinsed and drained chickpeas thoroughly on paper towels, and mix them in a bowl together with the baharat, salt and oil. Gently combine with your hands to ensure the chickpeas are evenly coated. Spread out on the lined baking sheet and bake in the oven for 40-50 minutes, turning regularly so they roast evenly.

Ultimate Bloody Mary with Harissa

The ultimate Bloody Mary! Cure a hangover and get a dose of vitamin C and one of your five a day all in one glass. As always, you can add more or less harissa, depending on how hot you want to go.

Makes 2–3

100ml (scant ½ cup) vodka
500ml (2 cups) tomato juice
1 tbsp lemon juice
Worcestershire sauce
Large pinch of sea salt
Large pinch of black pepper
½ tsp Harissa (page 26)
Ice cubes

Optional toppings
Celery sticks
Prawns
Gherkins
Olives
Fresh red chilli, minced
Chopped fresh parsley
Lemon wedges

Mix the vodka, tomato juice and lemon juice in a large jug or pitcher. Add a few dashes of Worcestershire sauce and the sea salt and black pepper. Add your harissa, tasting as you go to get your desired spiciness.

Half-fill two or three tall glasses with ice cubes and pour in the Bloody Mary.

Garnish with a celery stick for a more traditional finish, or get adventurous like I do and add prawns, gherkins, olives, chilli, parsley, and a wedge of lemon! And, when I'm really hungover... a burger on the side!

Espresso Martini with Ras el Hanout

This drink is perfectly balanced, but naturally I am going to include a spicy twist. The addition of ras el hanout totally elevates this classic drink and will make it even more memorable for anyone you serve it to. The recipe for the syrup makes more than you will need for one drink and so you can freeze what's left for use in the future.

Makes 1 serving

1½ tbsp Ras el Hanout Syrup (see below)
1½ shots (4½ tbsp) vodka
½ shot (1½ tbsp) coffee liqueur
1½ shots (4½ tbsp) espresso
Coffee beans, to garnish

Ras el hanout syrup
45g (1¾oz) sugar
5 tbsp water
½ tsp Ras el Hanout (page 27)

Put the ingredients for the ras el hanout syrup into a saucepan over a gentle heat. Warm through and simmer for 3-5 minutes until the sugar has dissolved, then turn off the heat and leave to steep for 15 minutes.

Fill a cocktail shaker with ice.

Once cooled, fine strain (best through a funnel lined with filter paper) 1½ tablespoons of your syrup into the shaker and add the vodka, coffee liqueur and espresso. Shake for 30 seconds until combined.

Pour into a Martini glass and garnish with the coffee beans.

Ras el Hanout Spiced Nuts

Sticky honey-roasted nuts, spiced to perfection, are the ideal snack for an evening chilling on the sofa or as a nibble for friends visiting for a beer.

Makes about 500g (1lb 2oz)

1 tbsp melted butter (or vegetable oil if you're vegan)
2 tsp Ras el Hanout (page 27)
500g (1lb 2oz) nuts (mixed or single variety)
2 tbsp honey (or maple syrup if vegan)

Preheat your oven to 140°C fan/160°C/320°F/gas mark 3.

Mix the melted butter with the ras el hanout in a large bowl. Carefully add the nuts and drizzle with half the honey. Spread over a baking (cookie) sheet and roast for 10 minutes, stirring halfway through.

After the 10 minutes is up, remove the nuts from the oven, drizzle with the remaining honey and cook for a further 10 minutes.

Remove from the oven and leave to cool, stirring the mix at least once to coat the nuts with the delicious spicy syrup on the baking sheet.

Divide into bowls and enjoy.

Spice Freedom

Harissa-spiced Popcorn

Ready to experiment with your blends? This recipe is equally amazing with: Ras el Hanout, Chinese Seven Spice, Gingerbread

My wife, Laura, always asks for this popcorn when we have a film night together. It's so easy and fun to make, and the house always smells sooooo good afterwards.

Makes enough for one, or for 2, if you can practise restraint!

3 tbsp sunflower oil
1 tsp Harissa (page 26)
50g (1¾oz) popcorn kernels
½ tsp salt
½ tsp paprika (optional)
1 tbsp melted butter

Heat the oil in a large, heavy-bottomed saucepan over a medium heat. Once hot, add the harissa blend and stir to infuse the oil. Let the harissa sizzle for 5-10 seconds, then add two popcorn kernels to the pan. Once they pop, quickly add the rest of the kernels. Move your saucepan away from the heat and give it a good shake. You want to do this for around 30-40 seconds, ensuring the kernels are moving but not shaking so vigorously that the kernels fly out! This prevents your popcorn from burning and also makes it cook evenly.

Place the pan back on the heat and pop a lid on it. You'll hear the lovely cacophony of popping for a while. Shake occasionally and when the popping slows down, remove from the heat. Tip the popcorn into a large bowl, sprinkle with the salt and paprika (if using) and drizzle over the melted butter.

Warming Mulled Wine/Apple Juice/ Cider

When I first started Spice Kitchen, I used to serve this at artisan markets throughout the winter to freezing customers who came to our stall. We quickly became known for serving the best mulled drinks around and I was totally blown away when the *Independent* newspaper declared them 'a triumph'. So, if you too want to be a triumph, give this recipe a go. The apple juice option is a great alternative for kids or non-drinkers and there is no need to add sugar. I promise everyone will love you for it.

Add the sugar to a large pan with the clementine juice and all of your spice blend. Gently pour in 100ml (scant ½ cup) of the wine/cider/apple juice and simmer very gently for 5 minutes. Add the remaining liquid and gently warm for a further 5 minutes. Strain into mugs and enjoy immediately.

100g (3½oz) sugar
Juice of 2 clementines
1 x 75cl bottle of wine, or 1 litre (4⅓ cups) cider or apple juice

Mulled spice blend
4g dried mixed peel
1g cardamom pods
1 stick cinnamon
1g whole black peppercorns
1g grated nutmeg
2 bay leaves, torn
1g whole cloves
2 star anise
½ tsp ginger powder

Makes enough for 4 drinks

In Our Kitchen

Over the years, Mum has passed down to me so many tips and tricks, shortcuts and recipes that have helped me to rustle up some amazing meals. It would require a whole new book for me to pass on everything she has taught me, so in this section I will share with you the tips and hacks that are relevant to dishes you will find in this collection.

The recipes that follow are those kitchen basics and staples that, once you get them nailed, are going to make your life so much easier, and your dishes that much more successful. You will save time, and money too, but more importantly, you're going to have some good skills up your kitchen sleeve.

Basic Bread Dough

There is no turning back from homemade bread. And it's so worthwhile to have a decent recipe up your sleeve, for the times when you can't be bothered to go to the shops! This one makes a really good batch quantity and freezes brilliantly.

Yield: This amount of dough is enough to make both the Harissa, Garlic and Coriander Swirl Bread (page 96) and the Spicy Za'atar Flatbreads (page 190).

15g (1oz) fresh yeast, or 7g (½oz/1 sachet) fast-action dried yeast
500g (1lb 10oz) very strong white flour, plus extra for dusting
2 tsp salt
2 tsp sugar
100ml (scant ½ cup) boiling water
200ml (1 cup) cold water
1 tbsp vegetable, sunflower or rapeseed (canola) oil

Place the sugar into a heatproof measuring jug (cup), add the boiling water to dissolve the sugar, then top up with cold water.

If using fresh yeast take a couple of tablespoons of your water and mix with the yeast to make a paste. Make the dough by tipping the flour and salt into a large bowl and, if using dried yeast. add it now.

Make a well in the middle of the flour mixture. Pour in the water/sugar mixture with the tablespoon of oil (if using fresh yeast add the paste now). Use a wooden spoon to mix until roughly combined.

Flour your work surface lightly and tip this mixture onto it; knead for at least 10 minutes until smooth and elastic.

Alternatively, if you have a mixer with a dough hook, combine all the ingredients in the mixer bowl as above and instead of tipping out, use the dough hook and turn it to the lowest setting to knead for 10 minutes.

You can freeze the dough at this point if you want to. See the instructions below.

Place the dough in a clean oiled bowl, cover with cling film (plastic wrap) and leave to prove until doubled in size.

The dough is now ready to be formed into a loaf or used to make other bread recipes. When you are ready to bake, grease a loaf tin and add your dough, then cook at 200°C fan/220°C/425°F/ gas mark 7 for 40 minutes. Allow to cool before turning out and carving a slice!

Freezing instructions

Brush the inside of a freezer bag with oil, place the dough in the bag, leaving space for the dough to rise a little as it freezes. You can keep it in your freezer until you're ready to use. To thaw the dough remove from the bag and place in a bowl or container with enough room for the dough to double in size and still not reach the top. Place in the fridge to defrost for 12-24 hours or until doubled in size, then remove from fridge and bring to room temperature. Shape and prove according to the recipe you are following.

Easy Midweek Naan

Mum never uses yeast in her naan bread. This self-raising (self-rising) flour option is super-fast and perfect when only fresh naan bread will do but you don't have a lot of time.

Makes 4

200g (7oz) self-raising (self-rising) flour,
   plus extra for dusting
½ tsp salt
2 tbsp vegetable, sunflower or rapeseed
   (canola) oil
100g (scant ½ cup) Greek-style yoghurt
50ml (3½ tbsp) water
1 tsp onion seeds (optional)
25g (1½ tbsp) butter, melted

Put the flour, salt, oil, yoghurt and water in a decent-sized mixing bowl. Mix together with your hand until you have one large ball of dough.

Lightly flour your work surface. Use some flour on your hands too, so the dough doesn't stick.

Flatten the dough and divide into four even portions. Sprinkle a little extra flour on top of the bread and then, using a rolling pin, roll out each portion to a thickness of about 5mm (¼in). At this stage, we like to add a sprinkling of onion seeds but it's up to you.

Heat a non-stick, heavy-bottomed frying pan (skillet) over a medium heat.

When your pan is hot, add one bread portion and cook for about 2-3 minutes on each side. You want them slightly coloured, but not burned.

Repeat until each bread is cooked.

As soon as you remove your bread from the pan, spread a little of the melted butter over the top for a gorgeously rich finish.

Easy Pizza Dough

I use this easy dough to make the Everyone's Happy Pizza on page 99.

Makes 6 pizzas

1kg (2lb 4oz) '00' (soft wheat) flour,
   plus extra for dusting
10g (¼oz) salt
4 tsp caster (superfine) sugar
10g Italian Seasoning (page 26)
14g (½oz) fast-action dried yeast (2 sachets)
6 tbsp olive oil, plus extra for greasing
600ml (generous 2½ cups) lukewarm water

Combine the flour, salt, sugar and Italian seasoning in a bowl. In a jug (pitcher), mix the yeast and olive oil into the measured water. Pour this into the flour and mix by hand to a shaggy dough.

Lightly flour your work surface, tip the dough onto it and knead for 5-10 minutes until smooth and elastic.

Clean the bowl out and grease it with olive oil. Return the dough to it and leave to double in size (about 1½-2 hours). You can freeze the dough at this stage for use later if you like or follow the cooking instructions for the dough in the Everyone's Happy Pizza recipe on page 99.

Big Batch Tomato Sauce

We're all busy people looking for ways to save time in the kitchen. Making a batch of tomato sauce can save the day when it comes to making your evening meals or throwing together a soup, stew or bolognese.

What I love about this recipe is that there are six fresh vegetables in it and yet, once it's all blended up, you'd never know. This means that you can easily get loads of vitamins and nutrients into your diets, and especially your children's without them realizing. This is also a great sauce to make use of any herbs left in your fridge or growing in your garden. A little rosemary, oregano, basil or marjoram will do no harm. Use what you have.

You'll find this tomato sauce used in many of our dishes in this book, including our Veggie Lasagne (page 161), Lamb-stuffed Aubergines (page 133) and Shakshuka (page 39), but you can make use of it in so many other ways.

Makes about 500ml (2 cups) sauce

3 tbsp olive oil
3 garlic cloves, peeled and minced
3 large red or white onions, peeled and
   finely chopped
2 aubergines (eggplants), trimmed and
   finely chopped
3 large carrots, trimmed, peeled and
   finely chopped
3 celery sticks, trimmed and finely chopped
2 (bell) peppers (red, orange or yellow or a
   combination), deseeded and finely chopped
2 tsp Italian Seasoning (page 26)
½ tsp salt
½ tsp freshly ground black pepper
800g (1lb 12oz) fresh tomatoes, diced
   or 2 x 400g (14oz) cans chopped or
   plum tomatoes
200ml (scant 1 cup) water

Optional
1 tbsp freshly chopped herbs
½ tsp Harissa (page 26)

You will need a large, lidded, heavy-bottomed frying pan (skillet).

Heat the olive oil in your pan over a medium-high heat. Once hot, add in the minced garlic and let it sizzle for 10 seconds, stirring to ensure it doesn't burn or stick to the bottom of the pan.

Then, add in all your veggies and give everything a good stir. Add the Italian seasoning, scrunching the herbs between your palms over the pan as you drop them in. This releases the oils and will make a difference to the end flavour. Add in the salt and pepper. Stir thoroughly again to combine.

Turn down the heat as far as it will go, pop your lid on and let everything cook for 30 minutes, or until the veggies start to colour slightly. Be sure to stir regularly. If the mixture is catching, you can add a splash of water.

Once your veggies have softened and taken on some colour, it's time to add your diced tomatoes (if you're using canned ones, be sure to break them up with a wooden spoon). Add in the water and turn up the heat until you get a good simmer going. If you are using any fresh herbs, now is the time to add them. You can also add the harissa blend if you would like your sauce to have a little kick.

When your sauce is bubbling, reduce the heat again and let everything cook for an hour or so. The sauce will reduce and thicken and the flavours will develop beautifully. If it becomes too thick, add more water.

Let it cool a little, then, using a stick blender, blitz to form a lovely smooth sauce. Taste, and season with salt and pepper if you think it needs more. Again, add a little more water if you think the sauce needs to be slightly thinner. It can be used immediately or you can cool then freeze it in individual portions ready for when you need some.

Tarka Sauce

This rich sauce can form the basis of so many curries, soups and stews. Cook up a big batch, freeze into portions and you can save yourself a whole heap of time. In this book, you will find it used in our Staff Chicken Curry (page 150), the Tarka Dal and Mamma Spice's Famous Chickpea Curry (both page 64).

Makes 1 litre (4⅓ cups)

5 tbsp vegetable, sunflower or rapeseed (canola) oil
3 garlic cloves, peeled and roughly chopped
1 tsp Tarka (page 28)
4 onions, peeled, halved and very finely sliced into half moons
1 tsp salt
2 tbsp Ginger-Garlic Paste (page 190)
2 tsp Garam Masala (page 26)
400g (14oz) canned plum tomatoes or 400g (14oz) tomatoes, finely chopped
1 tsp Harissa (page 26)
1 tsp turmeric (optional)

Place a large, lidded heavy-bottomed non-stick frying pan (skillet) over a medium heat and add your oil. Once hot, add in the roughly chopped garlic and the tarka. Allow the seeds to sizzle, pop and infuse the oil for about 30 seconds, being careful not to burn either the seeds or the garlic.

The following steps are crucial to the flavour and consistency of your sauce, so please don't rush or skip them:

Add the onions and salt to the pan and stir thoroughly to coat them in the oil. The salt will help the onions break down and form the base of your curry sauce, which is what you want. Fry them over a medium-low heat for about 5 minutes, stirring regularly, so they don't catch or burn.

After the 5 minutes, add your ginger-garlic paste, stir and continue to fry for a minute until the raw smell from the garlic has disappeared.

Next, add the garam masala, give the mixture another stir, then cook for about 20-25 minutes over a low heat. Every now and then, add a splash of water to the pan and bash the onions with a wooden spoon to break them down. The water will evaporate as you cook and you will begin to see the oil emerge again. You may need to adjust the heat throughout this process, turning up the heat a little when adding the water to get the pan and contents sizzling again. Eventually, your onions will turn into a thick paste-like consistency: this is when you will know they are done.

Add the canned or fresh tomatoes, breaking them up with the spoon, as well as the harissa and turmeric (if using). Stir thoroughly and then let the mixture cook for a further 15 minutes. The sauce will naturally thicken, so do add more water if you prefer a thinner consistency.

Taste and adjust the seasoning by adding more salt if you think your sauce needs it. You can also add a little more garam masala at this stage if it needs an extra boost of flavour.

If the sauce is to be used straight away, set aside and get cooking, but if not using immediately, let it cool then pop it into the fridge or freezer so that you can easily reheat when the time comes.

Perfectly Fluffy Rice

Say goodbye to claggy rice! I am going to share with you how to cook perfect rice every time using the absorption method.

There are so many different ways to cook rice, but we've always used the absorption method in my family. With a tiny bit of preparation and an understanding of how to get the best out of your ingredients, you can get perfectly fluffy rice every time you cook.

The absorption method works so well because it ensures you use the correct ratio of water to rice (2 cups water per 1 cup of rice), meaning that your rice won't need straining, is left perfectly cooked and is never claggy or starchy.

You will need good-quality basmati rice for the best results.

Serves 2–4, depending on the size of your cup. A serving of cooked rice is approximately 75g (2½oz) per person, so you can scale this up or down depending on how many you're cooking for.

Add 1 full cup of basmati rice to a non-metallic bowl. Fill the bowl with water and swirl the rice around in one single direction. You will see the water becomes cloudy.

Pour away the water and repeat the process twice more until the water is a little clearer. Pour the water away one last time, then add 2 full cups of fresh water to the rice.

Get out a wide, non-stick, heavy-bottomed saucepan with a well-fitting glass lid. This is super-important. Also, avoid using a pan that is liable to stick, as you don't want your rice to burn.

Turn on the heat to medium-high and add your rice and water to the pan, being careful to include all the grains stuck to the bowl.

Add 1 teaspoon of salt and put the lid on. Let the water come to a rolling boil and, as soon as it does, turn the heat down to its lowest setting.

Keep an eye on the pan and watch for when the lid is clear and you can see the rice through it, about 10 minutes. This means almost all the water is evaporated and there isn't any moisture left.

Turn off the heat and carefully remove the lid. You'll likely notice little wells or indents in the rice. You can gently part it and look to the bottom of the pan to see if there is any moisture left.

Pop your lid back on and let the rice sit for about 5-10 minutes, slowly cooking in its own steam.

Then, remove the lid and gently fluff it up with a fork. Serve immediately.

Variation: To make Sweet Rice - as served with our Rajma (see page 75) - follow the instructions above, but when you add your water to the pan, also add 4 green cardamom pods, a 2.5cm (1in) stick of cinnamon, 4 tablespoons of sugar and ¼ teaspoon of turmeric, if you have some.

Spicy Za'atar Flatbreads

These flatbreads are just lovely to pop on your table as part of a feast. They will be the perfect bread to mop up flavours and work amazingly with our simple Homemade Hummus (page 193).

Makes 10 flatbreads

Flour, for dusting
700g (1lb 9oz) risen white bread dough after its first prove (page 185)
4 tbsp Za'atar (page 28)
1 tsp Harissa (page 26)
½ tsp salt
3 tbsp olive oil

Preheat your oven to 220°C fan/240°C/475°F/gas mark 9 and place a baking tray (sheet) on the bottom shelf.

Flour your work surface and knock back the proved dough; leave to rest for 10 minutes.

Meanwhile, mix together the other ingredients.

Divide the dough into 10 equal pieces, each weighing 70g (2½oz).

When the oven is hot, roll two of the pieces into a teardrop shape or a circle if you prefer. If you want a thin crispy bread roll, go as thin as you dare, but if you want a softer, more pliable flatbread, roll until about 5mm (¼in) thick.

Carefully remove the baking tray and place the flatbreads on it. Return it to the bottom shelf of your oven and cook for 5 minutes.

Again, carefully remove the tray and sprinkle the top of each flatbread with the spice mix. Return to the oven for another 3 minutes, then remove and wrap in foil to keep warm.

Repeat the process until all the flatbreads are made. You can be rolling out the next two while the others cook.

Time-Saving Ginger-Garlic Paste

I have never known Mum to be without an ice-cube tray full of ginger-garlic paste in her freezer and a Tupperware container of the stuff in her fridge! It's such a staple in her kitchen that I'd think something was seriously wrong if she was ever without it.

It's so easy to make and will store for several months if you use a little oil and salt, so definitely worth spending a bit of time over the weekend getting a big batch made up in advance. Your midweek self will thank you! In many of the recipes in this book, you will see quantities of garlic and ginger separately; I don't want to presume you'll make the paste in advance but I hope you do. If you have made a stash then simply swap out the individual garlic and ginger for an equal quantity of this paste.

Makes about 250g (9oz) paste

125g (4½oz) fresh ginger
125g (4½oz) garlic cloves
½ tsp salt
1 tbsp vegetable, sunflower or rapeseed (canola) oil

Peel and roughly chop your ginger and garlic and add to your blender with the salt and oil. Blend until you have a smooth paste.

Either scoop into a clean jar or bottle and store in the fridge* or freeze in ice-cube trays and pop out a cube when you need to cook.

*Top tip: Your garlic may turn a little green (this happens when garlic is crushed and reacts with the air) but, don't worry, it's still absolutely fine to use.

Chinese Stock

Lu Ban restaurant in Liverpool kindly shared with us this master stock recipe. In China, this kind of stock recipe is revered and passed on as an art form, rather like how we might think of artisan breadmaking. Lu Ban's master stock is deeply aromatic and full of lovely ingredients and I feel so grateful that they have shared it with us for inclusion here.

The long simmer time ensures the stock is concentrated and will offer depth and a complexity of flavour to your dishes. In this book you will find it paired with Lu Ban's Crispy Duck recipe (page 136) but you can use it for braising or poaching any meat or tofu. Once cooled, it can be frozen and stored in the freezer for around 3 months.

Makes about 2 litres (8¾ cups) of stock, once reduced

2 tbsp Chinese Seven Spice (page 25)
1 lemongrass stalk, hard ends removed and
   roughly chopped
3 spring onions (scallions), roughly chopped
3 banana shallots, peeled and roughly chopped
3 garlic cloves, peeled and roughly chopped
1 small piece of fresh ginger, peeled and
   roughly chopped
3 tbsp vegetable, sunflower or rapeseed
   (canola) oil
230ml (scant 1 cup) Shaoxing wine
4 litres (4¼ quarts) cold water
20 black peppercorns
180ml (¾ cup) light soy sauce
200ml (scant 1 cup) dark soy sauce
300g (10½oz) sugar

Mix the Chinese seven spice with the lemongrass, spring onions, shallots, garlic and ginger. Put in a food processor with 2 tablespoons of the oil and blend to a smooth paste.

Heat the remaining oil in a large, heavy-bottomed saucepan, add the paste and cook until golden and crispy. Add the wine and stir.

Add the remaining ingredients to the pan. Allow to simmer for 1½-2 hours, skimming frequently. Once the cooking time is up, remove from the heat and pass through a sieve (strainer).

Use immediately or cool then freeze into portions until needed.

Dips and Chutneys

Homemade dips, pickles and chutneys offer so much to a meal. Mum's fridge and freezer is always stocked with dips made in advance and she has definitely taught me the virtues of doing the same. I've taken the time to provide you with a really comprehensive chapter on how to make some of our family favourites. I believe they will elevate your dishes and satisfy your tastebuds time and again. These recipes aren't an afterthought or a side; they're not something just to pop on the side of the plate but instead are pivotal to the flavour, texture and look of a meal. They are, in many ways, the main event. Get these right and your eyes, your tastebuds and your belly will thank you!

Homemade Hummus

Hummus is so lovely and also super-easy to make at home. You can use this recipe as a base and experiment by adding a teaspoon of any of the spice blends in this book for an exciting twist.

Enough for 4 as a side or dip

400g (14oz) can chickpeas (garbanzo beans), rinsed and drained
3 tbsp tahini
1 garlic clove
Juice of 2 lemons
Salt to taste
Olive oil, for drizzling

Blitz the chickpeas, tahini and garlic together, then add the lemon juice. Taste and season with salt. Dress with olive oil on the plate.

Easy Guacamole

I love it when such a tasty recipe has only four ingredients and a two-sentence description of what to do. The guacamole is the definition of simple. But make no mistake, it will also pack a punch thanks to the Mexican (Tex-Mex) blend.

Enough for 2 as a dip

1 large avocado, halved, pitted and peeled
Juice of 1 lime
1 tsp Mexican (Tex-Mex) blend (page 27)
Salt

In a large bowl, mash the avocado with the lime and season with the spice blend and salt. Cover and use immediately.

Harissa Mayo

Great for pimping up burgers, hot dogs and sandwiches. This harissa-spiced mayo is a great all-rounder: it takes less than 2 minutes to throw together and will become your go-to condiment for many years to come.

Enough to fill a medium-sized jar

250ml (generous 1 cup) good-quality mayonnaise (use plant-based if this is your preference)
1 tsp Harissa (page 26)
½ tsp garlic powder
½ tsp onion powder
Pinch of salt, to taste

Put all the ingredients into a large bowl and stir thoroughly to combine. Use immediately or transfer to an airtight container. It will keep in the fridge for up to 10 days.

Garlic Yoghurt

Tangy and fresh, this dip is the perfect side act to kebabs, burgers, prawns or as part of a feast.

Enough for 4 as a dip

200g (scant 1 cup) Greek-style yoghurt
1 tsp lemon juice
1 garlic clove, minced
1 tbsp fresh chives, finely chopped
Salt, to taste

Add all the ingredients to a large bowl and mix thoroughly. Serve immediately or cover and refrigerate until you're ready to use.

Janey's Crunchy Carrot Relish

This relish has been supplied to me for inclusion in this book by my good friend Janey. Janey's Crunchy Carrot Relish is famous; she made a whole business on the back of it. Sadly, Janey has decided to stop selling her relishes but said that including the recipe in this book was a way to keep the legacy alive! Janey gives the measurements in grams, and that's what I always follow because I want to ensure it's exactly as she says – it is THAT good.

It's the perfect relish to accompany chicken tikka and tandoori dishes or kebabs. It works wonderfully with hummus and many other vegetarian dishes. Equally, it's great with a hot curry and a bowl of yoghurt or simply as a dip with a pile of crispy poppadoms (pappadams). You'll find it in this book paired with our Spicy Lamb and Baharat Parcels (page 102).

Enough for about 8 small jars but easily scalable if you want to make less

28g Tarka (page 28)
5g nigella seeds
95ml vegetable, sunflower or rapeseed (canola) oil
45g garlic, minced
45g fresh ginger, minced
30g red chillies, chopped
4g ground turmeric (optional)
540g good-quality canned whole tomatoes, puréed
800g carrots, grated
360g apples, grated
5 tbsp cider vinegar
185ml water
100g sugar
50g tamarind pulp (widely available online and in most Asian supermarkets)
20g salt

Gently warm the tarka and nigella seeds in a dry pan until fragrant, then tip into a dish and set aside.

Next, select a saucepan big enough to hold all the ingredients. Heat the oil and add the garlic, then gently sauté until translucent.

Add the ginger and chillies and cook for 1 minute, then add the turmeric (if using). Cook for about 30 seconds, stirring as you do.

Next, add the tomatoes and then simmer this mixture gently for about 20 minutes until reduced and the oil begins to separate.

Add all of your remaining ingredients and cook for a further 10 minutes.

While your chutney cooks, sterilize your jars by rinsing them in hot water then popping them in the oven at 120°C fan/140°C/275°F/gas mark 1 for 10 minutes, or in a microwave on high setting for 30-45 seconds. Sterilize the lids by pouring boiling water over them and then leave to drain and dry on paper towels.

Fill the jars while the mixture is still hot and screw the lids on immediately. Use a clean dish towel or oven glove (mitt) to hold the warm jars.

Store in a cool dark place. The chutney will keep for up to a year unopened.

Pickled Red Onions

Great for perking up a salad or sandwich or for piling on a burger, these pickled red onions add a burst of flavour and a pop of colour to your dishes. They are super-easy to make and will keep for a fortnight in your fridge.

Enough to fill a medium-sized jar

3 red onions, halved and sliced
1 tsp black peppercorns (optional)
250ml (generous 1 cup) white wine vinegar
250ml (generous 1 cup) water
3 tbsp sugar
2 tbsp sea salt

Sterilise a jar big enough to hold your sliced onions (or a few smaller jars and divide the onions between them equally). Pop them in, together with the peppercorns (or a couple in each jar) if using.

Set a heavy-bottomed saucepan over a medium heat, add the rest of the ingredients and stir. The sugar and salt will begin to dissolve - this usually takes about a minute.

Allow the mixture to cool for a little while and then pour over your onions. If you are using several jars, be sure to allocate the liquid evenly. When the liquid has cooled completely, put the lid(s) on and store in your fridge.

Overnight, you will notice how magic happens, in that your onions will turn bright pink. This is when they are ready to add to your dishes.

Tartare Sauce with a Twist!

I made my own tartare sauce once and couldn't believe the difference in taste compared to what you buy in a jar. The 'twist' here is the mint, which, once you try, I promise you will never have this classic dip without it again.

Enough for 4 as a dip

1 tbsp drained capers
20g (¾oz) gherkins
6 tbsp good-quality mayonnaise (use plant-based if this is your preference)
Zest and juice of 1 unwaxed lemon
Leaves from 6 stalks of mint

Finely dice the capers and gherkins. Stir through the mayonnaise, then mix the lemon zest and juice through too. Finely shred the mint and fold it through. Keep in the fridge until you're ready to serve.

Za'atar Yoghurt

This yoghurt dressing is the perfect calming accompaniment to spicy koftes and kebabs.

Enough for 4 as a side

4 tsp Za'atar (page 28)
150g (5½oz) Greek-style yoghurt
4 garlic cloves, minced
Juice of ½ lemon
1 tsp salt

It's so easy: just mix everything together and serve over or alongside your dishes. This dip will also keep in the fridge for 3 days - transfer to a bowl, cover and refrigerate immediately.

Rainbow Slaw

Don't insult your tastebuds with shop-bought coleslaw when this recipe is so easy to throw together. I promise you'll never look back. In this book you'll find our rainbow slaw paired with the awesome Aloo Tikki on page 100 and the Fiery Blackened Cajun Chicken on page 72.

Enough for 4 as a side, depending on your portion sizes!

¼ red cabbage, shredded
2 medium carrots, peeled and grated
1 yellow (bell) pepper, seeded and sliced
1 red onion, peeled and finely sliced
¼ small celeriac (celery root), peeled and cut into matchsticks
3 tbsp Greek-style yoghurt
2 tbsp mayonnaise
½ tsp minced garlic
1 tbsp fresh parsley, roughly chopped (or fresh dill, leaves picked, if you have it), plus extra to serve
1 tsp English or Dijon mustard
Juice of ½ lemon
½ tsp salt
Freshly ground black pepper, to taste
1 tsp Harissa (page 26), optional, to serve

Add your prepared vegetables to a large bowl and stir to combine.

Then, add the yoghurt, mayonnaise, garlic, chopped herbs, mustard, lemon juice, salt and black pepper. Mix again to combine and taste, adding a little more salt and pepper if you think your slaw needs it.

Cover and put in the fridge until you're ready to serve, sprinkled with the extra chopped herbs and the harissa (if using).

Spiced Tomato Chutney

This chutney is so simple and it's perfect for using up any leftover fresh tomatoes and onions you have in your fridge. We like to use red onions because they keep the colour of the chutney a deep, rich and lovely red. You can also use this as a base chutney and experiment by adding a teaspoon of any of the spice blends in this book.

Enough to fill a medium-sized jar

3 red onions, peeled, halved and finely sliced into half-moons
500g (1lb 2oz) fresh tomatoes, roughly diced
1 tsp Harissa (page 26)
2 tbsp red wine vinegar
75g (2½oz) muscovado or brown sugar – whatever you have
½ tsp salt
Freshly ground black pepper, to taste

Put all the ingredients into a heavy-bottomed saucepan. Bring to a gentle simmer and then cook gently over a low heat for about 45 minutes, or until the tomatoes and onions have broken down and combined. Stir regularly to help this process and to ensure that nothing sticks to the bottom of the pan.

Allow the mixture to cool for an hour or so, then carefully spoon it into a sterlized jar (see page 194) with an airtight lid. Store in the fridge for up to a month.

Make this chutney work for you. Depending on how hot you want your chutney to be, you can add more or less harissa.

Fiery Salsa

Add freshness and a little fire to any dish with this flavourful salsa. It's definitely worth the extra time cooking the tomatoes and onions, to really bring out their sweet flavours. Remember to go up or down with the chillies depending on your heat preference. You'll find this dip paired with our Black Bean Nachos (see page 81).

Enough for 4 as a side

1 onion
4 garlic cloves
1–2 jalapeño chillies
5 plum tomatoes
Juice of 1 lime
Pinch of salt

First, make the salsa. Put the onion (in its skin), garlic cloves (in their papers), jalapeños and tomatoes in a heavy-bottomed frying pan (skillet).

Place the pan over a high heat and char everything all over. Alternatively, this can be done on a baking tray (sheet) in the oven at 180°C fan/200°C/400°F/gas mark 6, if you prefer.

Set aside to cool, then peel the onion and garlic cloves and pull the stems off the chillies (you can deseed them too, if you prefer).

Put the tomatoes, chillies, peeled garlic cloves and onion in a food processor and blitz.

Add the lime juice, taste, and season with salt.

Tamarind Chutney

Mum always has a stash of this in her freezer and will bring along a jar whenever she comes to visit. You can be like my mum, make a batch and freeze the sauce for when you need it. In our family, we like to make it quite sweet, but you can reduce the sugar and even use dates instead if you are more heath-conscious. In this book, you'll see our tamarind sauce used as a key feature of our Pav Bhaji recipe (page 87) but you can serve it with curries or samosas.

Makes around 300ml (1¼ cups) of sauce, enough to use with plenty left to freeze for later

250ml (generous 1 cup) water
300g (10½oz) sugar, or pitted dates if you prefer
½ tsp salt, to taste
½ tsp Harissa (page 26), to taste
200g (7oz) pack of dried tamarind (every Indian supermarket will stock this)

Place a large, heavy-bottomed saucepan over a medium heat. Add the water, sugar (or dates), salt and harissa. Break the tamarind into small pieces and add to the pan.

Bring to the boil and simmer for 8-10 minutes. The tamarind will begin to break down but you can help it along using the back of a wooden spoon.

After 10 minutes, turn off the heat and strain using a sieve (strainer) into a bowl. You'll be left with a gorgeous pulp in your sieve that's packed full of flavour. We want to get more flavour out of it, so don't throw it away. Instead, add a little water to the pulp (keep the bowl underneath) and keep mixing and adding a little more water and pushing the pulp through your sieve. If the pulp is cooled enough, you can even do this with your hands. Once you're happy you've squeezed all of the flavour out of the pulp, you can discard it.

You can then push the liquid through a finer sieve for a smooth consistency. Freeze in individual portions or serve immediately as a dip.

Zingy Mint and Coriander Chutney

Everyone who has ever tasted this chutney falls in love with it. I always try to keep a batch in my fridge and throw it over so many of my dishes, including sandwiches, wraps and Indian classics.

I know whenever my mum goes to the market, she's always on the lookout for the bigger bunches of herbs because she loves to make this chutney. It's super-easy and will add so much zing to your dishes. Using ice cubes when blitzing keeps your herbs bright green, so it will look amazing too. Here, we've used one chilli, but you can always add more or less, depending on your preference.

Enough to fill a medium-sized jar

50g (1¾oz) bunch fresh mint
50g (1¾oz) bunch fresh coriander (cilantro)
1 green chilli
1 tsp salt
2 tsp sugar
Juice of ½ lemon
6 ice cubes

Pick the mint leaves and discard the hard stalks. Roughly chop your coriander - you can use the stalks too as they will blitz down fine and add bags of flavour. Chop the end off your chilli and discard. Cut the rest into chunks, keeping the seeds.

Place in your blender, then add your salt, sugar, lemon juice and ice cubes.

Blitz for a few seconds until everything is combined and you have a lovely bright green chutney.

Spoon into a sterilized jar (see page 194) and keep in the fridge for up to a week or freeze into an ice-cube tray for when you need it.

Easy Tzatziki

This is another dip that tastes way better homemade than anything you'll buy in the shops. I like to eat this with some warmed pitta for a super-fast lunch. It's also a perfect way to cool down some of the more fiery dishes you'll find in this book.

Enough for 4–6 as a dip or a side

250g (1¼ cups) Greek-style yoghurt
1 medium cucumber, halved, seeded and coarsely grated
1 garlic clove, minced
2 tbsp extra virgin olive oil
½ tsp salt
¼ tsp black pepper
2 tbsp finely chopped fresh mint leaves, plus extra leaves to serve

Combine all your ingredients in a medium bowl, mix thoroughly and store in the fridge for 2-3 days. Add some extra fresh mint when you're ready to serve to fancy it up a bit.

Tahini Dressing

Possibly the easiest dressing to make in the world! I don't really need to say anything other than that.

Serves 2 as a dressing

2 tbsp tahini
Juice of ½ lemon
Splash of water
Pinch of salt, optional

Whisk together the tahini and lemon juice, adding a little water to thin it down. Season with a little salt.

Store in the fridge until you are ready to use. This will keep for up to 2 weeks.

Chimichurri

This takes 10 minutes to make and is amazing with grilled meat, veggies or as a dressing on a salad. In this book, you'll find this lovely accompaniment paired with our Spiced Peach and Goat's Cheese Salad on page 34 and the Tuna Steaks on page 130.

Serves 2 as a side

20g (¾oz) coriander (cilantro), finely chopped
20g (¾oz) parsley, finely chopped
2 garlic cloves, minced
1 shallot, very finely diced
½ tsp Harissa (page 26)
5 tbsp extra virgin olive oil
2 tbsp white wine vinegar
Pinch of salt

Add all the ingredients to a bowl and mix thoroughly. Taste for seasoning. It might need a little more salt, or more harissa.

Cover, and allow your chimichurri to sit for at least 10 minutes to let the flavours develop, but longer if you can (2-3 hours is perfect). For a looser consistency, you can add more olive oil.

Your chimichurri will keep in the fridge for up to 24 hours.

Flavour-bomb Harissa Paste

This paste is great to have in your fridge as it's so delicious and versatile: a few spoonfuls added to soups and stews will instantly liven them up and give them a Moroccan twist. It's perfect for making in advance and freezing. You will find this paste pumping up the heat in our Harissa, Garlic and Coriander Swirl Bread on page 96.

Enough to fill a medium-sized jar

1 red (bell) pepper
1 tbsp olive oil
1 small red onion, peeled and roughly chopped
3 garlic cloves, peeled and roughly chopped
3 tsp Harissa (page 26)
½ tbsp tomato purée (paste)
2 tbsp lemon juice
1 tsp lemon zest
½ tsp salt

Preheat your oven to 220°C fan/240°C/475°F/ gas mark 9.

Place the (bell) pepper in your hot oven until blackened on the outside and completely soft. Remove with tongs and place in a plastic freezer bag. Leave until cool enough to handle. Peel the pepper and discard its top, skin and seeds.

Heat the olive oil in a frying pan (skillet) over a medium heat and fry the onion until it is soft and just about to caramelize; then add the garlic and cook for another minute, stirring to ensure the garlic doesn't stick or burn.

Use a blender or a food processor to blitz together all of the ingredients until smooth, adding a little more oil if needed.

Store the paste in a sterilized jar (see page 194) in the fridge for 2 weeks or even longer.

Carrot and Cauliflower Pickle

If you make only one pickle from this book, make it this one: my mum's carrot and cauliflower pickle. I've been trying to perfect it for as long as I can remember and must confess that mine STILL isn't as good as hers, but it's pretty close. It will work well as a side for any of the Indian dishes in this book and is equally lovely served with poppadoms or naan. It will be fine in your fridge for a couple of weeks.

Enough to fill 1 large jar

2 tbsp vegetable, sunflower or rapeseed (canola) oil
1 tsp Tarka (page 28)
2 tsp Ginger-Garlic Paste (page 190)
2 green chillies, minced (remove the seeds if you want a milder pickle)
2 tsp Garam Masala (page 26)
½ tsp Harissa (page 26)
2 tsp salt
2 tbsp sugar
3 tbsp vinegar
Juice of ½ lemon
3 carrots, sliced into batons
1 small cauliflower, cut or broken into small florets

Heat the oil in a heavy-bottomed saucepan over a medium heat. Once hot, add in the tarka, ginger-garlic paste and green chillies. Cook gently for 1 minute, stirring regularly. Next, add the garam masala, harissa, salt, sugar, vinegar and lemon juice. Stir to combine.

Add the carrots and cauliflower, stir again and then turn down the heat to a simmer, cover and cook for 20 minutes until tender.

Turn off the heat and leave the pickle to cool down completely. Spoon into a sterilized jar/jars (see page 194) and store in the fridge until you are ready to use.

Harissa Kraut

My friend Jules at The Plucky Pickle used to keep my spirits up with her delicious Kimchi Grilled Cheese Toasties during long, cold days at Altrincham Market and I would repay her with a Masala Chai. She is literally the queen of fermentation and pickling, so you are going to love her tasty recipe, which Jules has generously offered for inclusion in this book. You should also check out her incredible fermentation masterclasses and online courses if this is something you are interested in, plus she has award-winning ferments to buy online.

Jules has made me promise to say that, before eating any fermented food or drink, always discuss with your GP first if you have any health or dietary requirements.

The classic kraut uses a process called dry salting, where you mix salt with shredded or grated vegetables (and fruits/spices/herbs if using) to create their own brine. It works on a ratio of 2 per cent salt to the weight of the prepped veggies. Try to shred the cabbage evenly, so there's not big chunks and smaller pieces, so everything can ferment consistently.

In this book, you'll find Jules's recipe paired with our Cajun-style Potato and Chorizo Hash (page 42). You can also get creative and try it with the Spiced Frittata (page 40) or add some of your brine to spritz up our Homemade Hummus (page 193).

Enough to fill a 1-litre (4⅓ cup) jar or other airtight vessel.

1 head of cabbage
2 garlic cloves, grated
A small finger of fresh turmeric, peeled and grated
1 generous tbsp Harissa (page 26)
Sea salt (use a good-quality one; for every 100g of prepped veggies you want 2g of salt)

Cut the cabbage into quarters. Save a few of the outer leaves - make sure they are in good condition. Cut the core out and chop the cabbage finely - you can use a food processor or mandoline for this.

Place a mixing bowl on a set of digital scales and set to zero. Add the chopped cabbage to the bowl, along with the grated garlic, grated turmeric and the harissa.

Note the weight. Calculate 2% of that weight for the amount of salt you need. So, if it's 1kg (2lb 4oz) you will need 20g (¾oz) salt. Add the salt to the bowl and massage it into the veg, distributing it evenly and squeezing the cabbage until you see a brine forming. Do this for about 10 minutes until you get a mound of limp, juicy cabbage.

Mix thoroughly. There should be a good amount of brine at the bottom of the bowl.

Pack the veggies tightly into a sterilized jar (see page 194), one handful at a time. Press down firmly on the cabbage mix until the brine rises to cover the veg, knocking out any air bubbles. Leave at least 2.5cm (1in) headspace at the top.

Take one of the whole cabbage leaves you saved to form a lid and place it in the top of the jar. Don't worry if this isn't fully submerged in the brine, as you will be disposing of this top leaf once everything has fermented.

If needed, put an additional small weight (say a clean jar lid or shot glass) on the top to keep the shredded veggies from floating to the top. Seal the jar.

Place on a plate or bowl in plain sight in your kitchen but out of direct sunlight and not near the cooker or radiator. It's super-important to keep this ferment anaerobic (without oxygen) and to ensure the cabbage mixture is fully submerged in its own brine.

Leave to ferment for a good 14 days minimum (I usually go up to a month in cooler weather). You will see bubbles inside the jar from about day 2 or 3, and brine may seep out a little. The amount of brine will increase - your ferment may get a little lively and start leaking juices due to gases building up during fermentation. Just gently 'burp' the kraut by opening the jar lid slightly every few days at the start, to allow excess gas to escape. Resist the temptation, though, to open the jar more than necessary, as you don't want oxygen getting in. The veggies must be under the brine and in an anaerobic environment.

Keep an eye on the kraut and refrigerate it when it is to your taste - it should be sour and tangy!

Lastly, don't ditch any leftover brine! Use it in salad dressings, dips, marinades, even cocktails. Add to homemade hummus to keep it a little longer and to brighten and give it a little sour kick.

Index

Gratitudes

This book would not have been possible without the support, encouragement, feedback and hard work of so many people behind the scenes.

Laura, the best wife I could have hoped for and the best mum to our beautiful daughter, Zara. Laura, you are my rock. You are the person who keeps me grounded and who has put up with spice madness for all of our married life. I could not have done this without you. Zara: I am proud of you in so many ways and I hope this book inspires you for a lifetime as you go on your own food journey. It's safe to say we have a foodie in you that we will nurture.

Mum and Dad, where do I even begin? You are the inspiration, the heart and the soul behind this book and behind everything I've ever achieved. Running Spice Kitchen with you both has been the most natural thing in the world to me and writing this book together has been the icing on the cake. The experience of a lifetime and something I will never forget. You are, without question, the definition of incredible and I am so blessed to have you as my parents. Mum: one day, you might actually realize how amazing you are. I hope this book nudges you a little closer to that thought.

Ann Lowe, you have been by my side for over a decade and none of this is possible without you. I am so glad we connected all those years ago; Spice Kitchen would have been a completely different business, and this cookbook would still be a pipe dream. From the tiny seed that was planted, it's quite incredible what you have helped me create in this wonderful book. I have definitely witnessed you go through all the emotions of being involved with this, but I loved watching your enjoyment of working on it. You bring an amazing balance of calmness and high energy in equal measure to everything you do. We have joked that you have put your whole life on hold to ensure this book was written, but I know this is actually the truth. I am truly blessed to have you beside me, in the team and also as a great friend.

Kate Young, you came out of nowhere and now I don't know where I'd be without you. You've been on the same page since the moment we first spoke, and your gentle encouragement, written support and recipe-testing need bigger praise than these words on a page. Thank you, thank you, thank you.

Our recipe collaborators: Hannah at Japan Centre, Hilina at Abyssinia Kitchen on the Wirral, Dave and the team at Lu Ban in Liverpool, Jules from The Plucky Pickle and Jane Fern, who have all contributed incredible recipes and who have believed in the power of spice blends! You have taken the time to create amazing dishes and drinks that are featured in this book and I will be forever grateful. We need to all get around the same dinner table one day.

Brad Doswell, our incredible mixologist who has developed, tried and tested many of the drinks recipes in this book, you are an absolute legend and I can't thank you enough for your wise words and support. You know you and Katie have all my love.

Lesley, Abi, Jessica, Georgina, Ros, Lyn, Andy, Duncan, Harry and Rob - and the rest of the amazing Spice Kitchen team who do all of the hard work packing spices and sending them out to our customers. Without your presence, dedication, support and passion for this business, I would be a lost, balding crazy man with just a silly idea about selling spices. I can cope with just being bald. You have no idea just how much I appreciate and value you all.

Elaine of Foodbod Sourdough, you have supported me for years, and your encouragement has enabled me to take so many steps forward in life, in business and in the writing of this book. I am so glad we met; you are a guiding light in this world. We bonded over spices all those years ago and I am so inspired by what you have created in the sourdough world. I value our friendship immensely.

Big thanks to my Uncle Paul for teaching me how to cook the perfect roast and for being my second foodie mentor after my mum!

My friends Pete, Helena, Jimmy, Ruth, Zee, and Chevs for tasting, feeding back and testing recipes with me and generally being amazing and supportive. I love you all.

Nicola at Dishoom, for your support, encouragement, wise words and lovely food all along this journey! I have always been inspired by Dishoom and you. And also massive thanks for giving us Kate.

Clare Hulton, our amazing literary agent who held our hand from the start and who has been professional, supportive and so knowledgeable all the way through.

Huge thanks to the absolutely amazing creative team who helped bring this book to life. Dan, your food photography is beyond what I could have ever imagined and I can't believe how beautiful you've made everything. And also to Jodene, the incredible food and props stylist who is so so talented and so grounded and humble all at the same time. A million thank yous!

Sophie, Sarah, Claire and all at Quadrille Publishing. You have been amazing to work with, so helpful, so approachable and so deeply human. It has been an utter joy. We have felt massive imposter syndrome, especially compared to all the other great chefs and cooks you guys have worked with. Thank you for taking a chance on us and believing in what we were trying to achieve, and for your continued patience and guidance along the way.

Sanjay Aggarwal runs Spice Kitchen, an award-winning, artisan spice and gift company founded by Sanjay and his mother Shashi Aggarwal. The business was initially set up as a retirement project for Shashi. On Christmas Day in 2012, they were chatting over the dinner table, and Shashi said she wanted to do something meaningful with her spare time. Sanjay suggested that she start selling traditional Indian Spice tins. So the pair sat together and made a tin. Sanjay took a photo, listed it on eBay, and to their surprise, it sold on Boxing Day. Spice Kitchen was born.

Fast-forward to the present day, Spice Kitchen has grown beyond their wildest imagination. Sanjay and Shashi carefully hand pick only the highest quality spices, manufacturing blends in-house to ensure freshness and flavour. It has won three Great Taste Awards and has appeared in the media numerous times.

spicekitchenuk.com @spicekitchenuk

Managing Director
Sarah Lavelle

Project Editor
Sophie Allen

Head of Design
Claire Rochford

Photographer
Dan Jones

Food & Props Stylist
Jodene Jordan

Head of Production
Stephen Lang

Production Controller
Sabeena Atchia

Quadrille, Penguin Random House UK,
One Embassy Gardens, 8 Viaduct Gardens,
London SW11 7BW

Quadrille Publishing Limited is part of the Penguin Random House group of companies whose addresses can be found at global.penguinrandomhouse.com

Published by Quadrille in 2023

www.penguin.co.uk

A CIP catalogue record for this book is available from the British Library

ISBN 978 1 78713 939 8
10 9 8 7 6 5 4 3

Colour reproduction by F1

Printed in China by C&C Offset Printing Co., Ltd.

The authorised representative in the EEA is Penguin Random House Ireland, Morrison Chambers, 32 Nassau Street, Dublin D02 YH68.

Penguin Random House is committed to a sustainable future for our business, our readers and our planet. This book is made from Forest Stewardship Council® certified paper.